GUIDELINES FOR CONTEMPORARY CATHOLICS

Life, Death and Science

GUIDELINES FOR CONTEMPORARY CATHOLICS

Life, Death and Science

Richard Westley

THE THOMAS MORE PRESS
Chicago, Illinois

Grateful acknowledgment is made to Twenty-Third Publications, P. O. Box 180, Mystic, CT 06335, for permission to reprint passages from *A Theology of Presence* by the author of this book, Richard Westley.

ISBN 0-88347-232-5

TABLE OF CONTENTS

PREFACE

A RECENT news story filled me with horror and the realization that we humans have become so insensitive to the sacredness of life and love and birthing that we remain silent in the face of even the most outrageous profanation. East Germany has invested its national image heavily into sports and sports medicine. Their accomplishments in competition have been very impressive. So it was not surprising that once they discovered a woman's muscles are at their best and most efficient during pregnancy, someone there came up with the idea to have their woman athletes be pregnant for the Olympics, and then have them all abort after the games.

A second recent news story filled me with consternation. A couple was reported to have made the decision to bring an anencephalic fetus (one with no higher brain structures, just a brain stem) to term. They wanted to then donate the organs of their child, fated to die within two weeks after birth, to "give life" to other children. My consternation arose from the fact that the government, the church and the medical profession all seemed to be firmly against such an idea.

Something is certainly radically wrong with our world. The gift of life was being rejected as somehow immoral or inappropriate, and yet no great hue and cry was sent up over the proposal of the East Germans. It was reported on the news with cool and detached objectivity.

In the light of those, and similar, events, perhaps it is time for us to stop and to reflect on just where we are with regard to such matters and to assess, if we can, the principles behind the Catholic position. I have tried to do just that in this little book. Chapter One attempts to describe the context of modern day medicine and the new life/death technologies. Chapters Two and Three present the traditional Catholic view of morality, and some contemporary attempts at its updating and revision. Chapter Four considers the pros and cons of the new reproductive technologies, and Chapter Five does the same for other life/death issues.

My special thanks go to Joel Wells and Thomas More for so graciously accepting the delays I encountered along the way.

Richard Westley

CHAPTER ONE
Context of the Problem

1. *A Question of Limits*

THOUGH this book is entitled *Life, Death and Science,* it is really a book about something we generally don't like to talk about—limits. The new developments in science and medical technology have once again seriously raised the question as to whether our ability to do some things which have great potential to benefit human beings is alone sufficient warrant for our actually doing them. Common sense would seem to indicate that if a medical technology is of real and substantial benefit to human beings then it most certainly ought to be practiced. But our common sense also warns us against being too quick to accept the promise of great benefit from those whose primary goal is really personal profit. Indeed, profit-making itself raises the problem of limits. Is there any sort of limit not only on how much money a person can make at a given enterprise, but more significantly on the kinds of activities it is appropriate for human beings to engage in for money's sake? If limits there be on such things, how does one go about determining what they are, at what point in the enterprise they come into play, and what we are to do, in a pluralistic society, when men and women of good will don't agree on the matter?

We have come to depend on science. No. We have come to

depend so on science that our lives are unthinkable without it. Science represents freedom and opportunity to us, as we compare our lives with those of women and men in ages past. Without science our lives would be no better than theirs, and we would lose the feeling that we are indeed living in a privileged time: The Age of Science. We envy those who will come to life in the twenty-first or twenty-second centuries because we are convinced their lives will be even more privileged and exciting than our own.

Science and technology have not only contributed wondrous "things" to enhance our lives, the many inventions and conveniences which mark our age, they have made even more wondrous contributions to life itself, enabling the transplantation of organs, the overcoming of infertility, the dissemination of wondrous drugs and vaccines, the control of the major diseases which plagued our ancestors, neo-natal, micro and open heart surgery, as well as knee and hip replacements to mention only a few of the medical marvels of our time. These tangible results of scientific research in current medical practice have filled us with awe, and raised our expectations to heights once thought unattainable. Our only sorrow and lament is that we were perhaps born too soon to take fullest advantage of the projected new marvels just over our present horizon. Those who in any way question the right-headedness of such progress are seen at best to be hopelessly tied to the past, at worst to be somewhat demented.

That was pretty much the state of affairs until the late 50's when James Watson and Francis Crick discovered the structure of DNA, unlocking the secrets of living matter and ushering in the mind-boggling biological revolution of our times. To date, we have only experienced the tip of the iceberg, but even conservative projections predict nothing less than a transformation of human life which will make the Industrial and Electronic revolutions pale to insignificance. Much as was the case most recently with electronics, new businesses are springing up around the new biomedical technologies, pursuing ever greater human control of life itself and the consequent wealth such control will most certainly generate. The drive of this biological revolution daily gains increased momentum making it appear unstoppable, and the transformed world it promises, inevitable.

It is against this backdrop of a new "gold rush," with all its accompanying chaos and destruction, that the voices of the church, of believers and humanists of every persuasion, and even of the more sensitive scientists themselves, are once again raising the urgent question of limits.

In his marvelous little book *Who Is Man?,* Rabbi Heschel makes the important distinction between "human being" and "being human," and speaks of the relation between them.[1] In the end, he identifies human being as a fact, indeed a biological one. One is a member of the genus *homo sapiens* on the proviso that one has a specific genetic code. Thus one is a "human being" if one's cells have the specifically human structure, a certain configuration, as it were, of DNA. On this account, one cannot do anything to become a "human being." It either describes one's biological make-up or it doesn't. One had absolutely no role in acquiring this "biological" humanness, it is a given which one either has or does not have from conception. Thus "human being" is in the realm of brute fact.

But that biological "humanness" is a kind of humanness after all. That is to say it demands and cries out for "being human," which goes beyond the realm of biological fact. "Being human" depends on certain freely chosen relations without which one will cease to be human. "Human being" is a fact, but "being human" depends on certain sensibilities and the modes of response each of us chooses to the world around us, to our fellow human beings, and to that which "is" but is never directly given, i.e. the transcendent.

That means that we can determine whether someone who has the proper biological structure to be a "human being" is also "being human" by the way that person responds to the realities that surround her. But Heschel gives a second way of determining whether one is "being human." Since "being human," as spiritual, transcends the mute givenness of "human being" by not being satisfied with its biological facticity, we are able to discern the quality of "being human" in all the ways we humans have of transcending the given. That is to say, by the kinds of things we ourselves "bring into being," or "add to reality," our own special and unique contributions to the world. Heschel identifies four such additions as: our thoughts, the things we make, our deeds, and most importantly, our offspring.

If the test to check for "human being" is a biological one, i.e. an examination of the genetic code in each of our cells, the test for "being human" is more subtle but no less accurate. One's "humanness" is judged by the way she relates, and by the contributions she makes, to reality.

Obviously having the Holocaust in mind, Heschel muses that this distinction between "human being" and "being human" gives rise to a frightening possibility. The earth could well be peopled by those who qualify as "human beings" because of their biology, but who are devoid of those sensibilities and modes of response which distinguish the members of the human race from all the rest of creation. All those who ran the concentration camps were undoubtedly human, biologically speaking. But the depth of their dehumanization can easily be judged by their relations with the inmates, and by the kinds of things they introduced into our world. The ovens and gas chambers remain to this day silent but eloquent witnesses of just how far dehumanization can go, and at what a price. Heschel concludes that humankind must therefore remain ever on guard, not only to ward off all those things which could lead to the biological extinction of "human being," but must also be constantly vigilant against dehumanization, which is the spiritual extinction of "being human." It is a fatal illusion to think that to protect the former is automatically to protect the latter.

For Heschel[2], one of the most significant modes or signs of "being human" is our sensitivity to what is sacred, defining "sacred" as a sort of limit. The sacred is that in the presence of which we feel our own finitude, and have the experience that here, at least, we are face to face with something over which we cannot *properly* exercise our wills. To ignore that experience of limit, to proceed to prostitute the sacred for one's own interests is what we mean by "profanation." To be truly "human," we must have that sensitivity toward the sacred, and must, in Heschel's words, be willing to accept the existential paradox of "saying 'yes' to a 'no'." To the degree that we are either unwilling or unable to do that, to that same degree we lack something essential of what it takes to "be human," and that seemingly slight dehumanization, like a cancer, begins to eat away at and skewer the way we relate to our world, and the kinds of things we are capable of adding to it. Consequently, our "being human" is at risk of extinction, not from outside forces, but from within our very selves. Are we willing to accept that there are some things which are "sacred," things we simply cannot prostitute to self-interest without dehumanizing ourselves? And even if we accept that fact and live it, precisely where is that limit to be drawn?

2. *Contemporary Doctors vs. Traditional Physicians*

Respect for the limit, the sacredness of human life, has marked the medical profession from its earliest days. While in every age there have always been medical practitioners who have not lived up to the highest canons of their profession, there have also always been, in every age, professional canons and public codes of conduct which sought to speak to the special nature of the patient/physician relationship. Perhaps the most influential of such codes was the Hippocratic Oath, which, until the mid-twentieth century, was administered, in modified form, to the students of medical schools on graduation day.

Hippocrates, a Greek physician from the fourth century B.C., sought to separate the practice of medicine from the traditions of the religion, magic and superstitions of his day. He denied that disease was due to supernatural influence and urged the use of the powers of human observation in diagnosing and treating the sick. Whether it was Hippocrates himself who wrote the famous oath that bears his name is uncertain, but it came to be included among his works. Of whatever origin, it clearly demonstrates the sensitivity to limits of which we have been speaking. It reads:

Life, Death and Science

The Hippocratic Oath

"I swear by Apollo Physician and Asclepius and Hygieia and Panaceia and all the gods and goddesses, making them my witnesses, that I will fulfill according to my ability and judgment this oath and this covenant:

To hold him who has taught me this art as equal to my parents and to live my life in partnership with him, and if he is in need of money to give him a share of mine, and to regard his offspring as equal to my brothers in male lineage and to teach them this art—if they desire to learn it—without fee and covenant; to give a share of precepts and oral instruction and all the other learning to my sons and to the sons of him who has instructed me and to pupils who have signed the covenant and have taken an oath according to the medical law, but to no one else.

I will apply dietetic measures for the benefit of the sick according to my ability and judgment; I will keep them from harm and injustice.

I will neither give a deadly drug to anybody if asked for it, nor will I make a suggestion to this effect. Similarly I will not give to a woman an abortive remedy. In purity and holiness I will guard my life and my art.

I will not use the knife, not even on sufferers from stone, but will withdraw in favor of such men as are engaged in this work.

Whatever houses I may visit, I will come for the benefit of the sick, remaining free of all intentional injustice, of all mischief and in particular of sexual relations with both female and male persons, be they free or slaves.

What I may see or hear in the course of the treatment or even outside of the treatment in regard to the life of men, which on no account one must spread abroad, I will keep to myself holding such things shameful to be spoken about.

> If I fulfill this oath and do not violate it, may it be granted to me to enjoy life and art, being honored with fame among all men for all time to come; if I transgress it and swear falsely, may the opposite of all this be my lot."[3]

It is clear why this statement of principles should have become the cornerstone of the medical profession for two millennia. It is also clear why it does not represent the mind of the health care community today. Apart from its Greek religious overtones, its seeming condemnation of surgery, abortion and euthanasia make it problematic in the minds of many. But I think it remains a remarkable account of the mind set of one who aspires to be *physician.*

By contrast, one does not get that same sort of feeling when reading of the American Medical Association Code for 1980. One recognizes at once that she is in a different world. There are *traces* of the former respect for patients, but there are also some statements which seem to open the door to using patients for some other end or higher purpose. Indeed, commitment and respect for one's individual patients is replaced by a more general commitment to humanity in general. This opens the door to using the patient in front you for the common good of the rest of humanity. The bond between physician and patient, while still spoken of with great respect, does not have the same sacredness as was evident in the now discarded Hippocratic Oath. More concerned with the contemporary passion to mollify paternalism, delineate the "rights" of physicians and patients, and to establish the freedom of the physician to do scientific research, it reads:

Life, Death and Science

American Medical Association
Principles of Medical Ethics, 1980[4]

The medical profession has long subscribed to a body of ethical statements developed primarily for the benefit of the patient. As a member of this profession, a physician must recognize responsibility not only to patients, but also to society, to other health professionals, and to self. The following Principles adopted by the American Medical Association are not laws, but standards of conduct which define the essentials of honorable behavior for the physician.

I. A physician shall be dedicated to providing competent medical service with compassion and respect for human dignity.

II. A physician shall deal honestly with patients and colleagues, and strive to expose those physicians deficient in character or competence, or who engage in fraud or deception.

III. A physician shall respect the law and also recognize a responsibility to seek changes in those requirements which are contrary to the best interests of the patient.

IV. A physician shall respect the rights of patients, of colleagues, and of other health professionals, and shall safeguard patient confidences within the constraints of the law.

V. A physician shall continue to study, apply and advance scientific knowledge, make relevant information available to patients, colleagues, and the public, obtain consultation, and use the talents of other health professionals when indicated.

VI. A physician shall, in the provision of appropriate patient care, except in emergencies, be free to choose whom to serve, with whom to associate, and the environment in which to provide medical services.

VII. A physician shall recognize a responsibility to participate in activities contributing to an improved community.[5]

The bond between patient and physician has changed dramatically, no doubt accounting to some significant degree for the increased number of malpractice suits in our time. Thus, the patient-physician relationship has in our time been eroded of the trust which had always marked it from the beginning.

Today we are less likely to talk about "our doctor" (the family's physician) or "my doctor," but about "*the* doctor," a good indication of the changing patient/physician relation. We seem to want it that way, since we know how much science and medicine have advanced. We insist on having our health care people competent and knowledgeable, and consider it something of a surprising bonus should they also turn out to be care-filled and genuine healers. At least that is the way we feel *before* our operation, or our visit to the office. Afterward, we wish that the high level of competence we expect could be found in someone with a bit more sensitivity to the "human" dimension of things. Someone whose value system gave us reason to be more trusting. In any event, precisely at the time we are most vulnerable and in need of the help of others, we feel terribly distanced from those to whom we must entrust ourselves for healing. It is therefore all too easy to have recourse to the courts when things go wrong, something unthinkable when the relations with the physician were more intimate and humane. But we cannot really blame the health care professionals for the situation, they are as much the victims of it as we are; besides they could justifiably reply that they are merely responding to what we say we want.

Still, as the health care professionals implement more and more of the findings of modern science into their work, medical practice looks more and more like a business and less and less like a profession. Hospitals which were once places of genuine hospitality for those in need are being taken over by corporations and efficiency experts, on the excuse that all the new technology is so costly that it necessitates some such move. Health care costs are out of sight for those who have insurance, and out of reach for those who don't. Corporate profits and medical income have reached unheard-of heights, but then so too have malpractice insurance and the costs of medical education. Technology does medical marvels, but it also generates great wealth. Who is to say what is really motivating us to keep on the track of ever greater and more startling technology?

In such circumstances, people are beginning to seriously question the right-headedness of the current health care delivery system, and one of the greatest fears people experience these days is that they may get sick and fall into the hands of the impersonal, but ever more competent, health care system. The cry is going up across the land for a re-evaluation of the priorities of the health care professions. Where does the patient fit into the picture with the other goals of present day medical practice? As we more and more have come to look on health care as a commodity like any other, the costs of medical care have increased exorbitantly. We think it is worth it, but can't help wondering where we fit into the picture when the primary goal seems to be making money and/or advancing science. The question of limits and the sacredness of each individual life is being raised once again with renewed urgency. And as is so often the case in such situations, we look for help from the institutions most vested in traditional practice. In the matter of the sacredness of life, the meaning of death, and the proper limits for human conduct that means looking to the government, especially the judicial branch, to the governing bodies of the health care professions, to the universities, as well as to faith communities and the churches. But in our present day secular environment, not much is hoped for from these latter sources, it being assumed in advance that churches will by and large merely repeat the outmoded values of the past, not taking modern advancements sufficiently into account.

3. *Church, the Tradition, and the Current Situation*

The reality and depth of present concern can be judged by the fact that there has been, in the past 20 years, an ever increasing interest in medical ethics. The government has set up committees to advise the medical profession on ethical matters, colleges and universities have added courses in medical ethics to the curriculum, hospitals have ethics committees to monitor and advise the medical staff on the ever more difficult ethical decisions which the new technology has precipitated, and some have even hired their own resident ethicists. Given the projected effects of the current biological revolution, these sorts of efforts are bound to intensify, as new technologies impose greater and ever more difficult ethical decisions on us all.

Unlike the latecomers to such concerns, the Catholic church has from the start warned us against the creeping dehumanization of our secular age. As religion was replaced by business at the heart of American life, the tendency and inclination toward dehumanization increased.[6] Often this did not seem important, since secularization seemed to offer immediate and evident benefits of increased leisure, wealth and power. While the world continued on its secular way, the Catholic Church was always there challenging the values and assumptions which form the foundations of contemporary secularism.

One would think that that track record would make us more inclined to listen to the church now that science and the new technologies prepare more and greater dehumanizations for us all in the name of progress. But the fact is that the great strength of the Catholic Church as a champion of the human, is perceived by many as also its fatal weakness. How can an institution which is so committed to a fixed ideology be open enough to fairly assess current developments? In order to keep faith with its own traditions, it has no choice, some say, but to approach the new advances with a closed mind. It can not do otherwise than to reject them.

Thus, no one was surprised by the 1987 document issued by the Sacred Congregation for the Doctrine of the Faith regarding respect for human life.[7] Many judge that it is just the same old thing. In many respects, that is true, but that leaves unanswered whether the same old thing happens to be true or not. If it is, then it is of no significance that it is the "same" or "old," because when something is "old" *and* "true," that can only mean that it is wise.

That the Catholic church has been truly wise on the life-death issues over the centuries cannot be denied. It matters not at all that often her wisdom is not recognized as such and rejected as old fashioned. When it comes to the life-death issues, the

Catholic church has always been there urging the sacredness of human life and an acceptance of appropriate limits. Were that all that need be said on the matter, there would be no sense in writing this book. The fact is the Catholic church has not always exhibited that same kind of wisdom with regard to the issue of science. One need only recall the Galileo (1564-1642) case to be convinced of it. Only recently, in 1984 after three and a half centuries, has the church released the documents of the trial suggesting that the court hearing the case had been in error.[8] Stated that way, it could be interpreted to mean that the court was in error but the church was not. That sort of rhetoric gives thoughtful persons reason to pause, as well as reason to question the credibility of the Catholic church when it comes to science.

Its credibility has suffered, too, from its positions on sex and human reproduction. Ever since the issuance of *Humanae Vitae*[9], Catholics have been sorely divided within the church on sexual issues. And amid all the turmoil over such things, there is the overlay of the women's issue, which poses, perhaps, the most serious challenge to Rome's credibility in our times. So despite its centuries-long record of wise counsel in behalf of human dignity and the issues of life and death, the voice of the Catholic church still remains suspect, in many quarters, on issues of science and technology, and especially on the issues of human reproduction, necessarily freighted with the overlay of the women's issue.

Faced with hostility or indifference from without, the voice of the Catholic church, even when it speaks wisdom, is not taken as seriously as it should be. And this precisely at a time when the discussions of limits with regard to life-death issues and the new biological technologies is in desperate need of wise counsel. But there is more.

Within the Catholic church at this moment in history there is a raging controversy among moral theologians as to whether or not the Catholic moral tradition has indeed been interpreted correctly. At stake is whether the official interpretation of the traditional natural law approach to life-death issues is the correct one. Cautious and careful work by a group of theologians called "revisionists" or "proportionalists" has called the traditional interpretation into question.[10] Their work has so challenged traditional thinking, that every month there are new rumors predicting that Rome will have to issue some sort of statement condemning their approach and its results. Reliable sources keep saying that such a move is definitely in the works.[11] I only mention that because it shows that this is a very propitious time to consider, compare and contrast the traditional and revisionist approaches to determining the morality of an act, and then to see what, if any, difference that makes in handling the pressing moral issues precipitated by the new biology from the perspective of faith.

NOTES TO CHAPTER I

1. Abraham Heschel, *Who Is Man?,* Stanford Univ. Press, 1965, cf. pp. 10, 16, 29, 41.

2. *Ibid.*, p. 48.

3. As cited in Edwards & Graber, *Bio-Ethics,* Harcourt Brace Jovanovich, New York, 1988, p. 40.

4. *Ibid,* p. 41.

5. It is instructive to compare the AMA statement of 1980 with the one of 1957, to see how much the later statement reflects the tenor of our times. The 1957 statement reads:

American Medical Association Principles of Medical Ethics (1957)

"These principles are intended to aid physicians individually and collectively in maintaining a high level of ethical conduct. They are not laws but standards by which a physician may determine the propriety of his conduct in his relationship with patients, with colleagues, with members of allied professions, and with the public.

1) The principal objective of the medical profession is to render service to humanity with full respect for the dignity of man. Physicians should merit the confidence of patients entrusted to their care rendering to each full measure of service and devotion.

2) Physicians should strive continually to improve medical knowledge and skill, and should make available to their patients and colleagues the benefits of their professional attainments.

3) A physician should practice a method of healing founded on a scientific basis; and he should not voluntarily associate professionally with anyone who violates this principle.

4) The medical profession should safeguard the public and itself against physicians deficient in moral character or professional competence. Physicians should observe all laws, uphold the dignity and honor of the profession and accept its self-imposed disciplines. They should expose, without hesitation, illegal or unethical conduct of fellow members of the profession.

5) A physician may choose whom he will serve. In an emergency, however, he should render service to the best of his ability. Having undertaken the care of a patient, he may not neglect him; and unless he has been discharged he may discontinue his services only after giving adequate notice. He should not solicit patients.

6) *A physician should not dispose of his services under terms or conditions that tend to interfere with or impair the free and complete exercise of his medical judgment and skill or tend to cause a deteriorization of the quality of medical care.*

7) *In the practice of medicine a physician should limit the source of his professional income to medical services actually rendered by him, or under his supervisions, to his patients. His fee should be commensurate with the service rendered and the patient's ability to pay. He should neither pay nor receive commission for referral of patients. Drugs, remedies or appliances may be dispensed or supplied by the physician provided it is in the best interests of the patient.*

8) *A physician should seek consultation upon request; in doubtful or difficult cases; or whenever it appears that the quality of medical service may be enhanced thereby.*

9) *A physician may not reveal the confidences entrusted to him in the course of medical treatment, or the deficiencies he may observe in the character of patients, unless he is required to do so by law or unless it becomes necessary in order to protect the welfare of the individual or of the community.*

10) *The honored ideals of the medical profession imply that the responsibility of the physician should not extend only to the individual, but also to society, and these responsibilities deserve his interest and participation in activities that have the purpose of improving both the health and well-being of the individual and the community."*

Journal of the American Medical Association, Vol. 164 #10, (July 6, 1957), pp. 1119-1120.

6. For an enlightening and provocative account of the state of present day American culture cf. Robert Bellah, *Habits Of The Heart,* Harper & Row, New York, 1985.

7. *Instruction On Respect for Human Life in its Origin and On the Dignity of Procreation: Replies To Certain Questions of the Day,* Congregation for the Doctrine of the Faith, 1987. Publication No. 156-3 of the Office of Publishing and Promotion Services, United States Catholic Conference, Washington D.C.

8. See articles for March 18, 1984 and July 22, 1984 in *The National Catholic Register,* Vol. 60, #3.

9. The famous ''birth control'' encyclical. Paul VI, *Humanae Vitae,* Rome, July 25, 1968.

10. Cf. Chp. III, Note #3.

11. I can't help wondering whether the delay in coming out against so-called ''proportionalism'' is not partly motivated by the fact that the revisionists have been so persuasive in their scholarship that to do so would mean coming out against Thomas Aquinas, himself. That could prove to be very awkward, since Aquinas' moral theory is such an integral part of the Catholic moral tradition.

CHAPTER TWO
Traditional Catholic Morality

IN everyday circles and ordinary language, the phrase "Catholic morality" refers to the code of conduct officially taught by the Catholic Church, violations of which are publicly designated as "immoral acts" or as "sins." Generally, these two terms are taken to be synonyms, but as I have tried to show elsewhere, they really are not.[1] To be convinced of it, one has only to reflect on the fact that we are well aware that we mean something different when we say of an act that it is "immoral" and that it is a "sin." When we say something is a sin, we do not expect that every human person would agree with us, because "sin" is a faith or theological term which factors in one's own religious perspective and assumes the existence and presence of God, but many do not believe in God at all. And even among believers, sometimes, but not always, what is a "sin" to a Moslem, a Hindu, a Jew and a Christian will be quite different. On the other hand, when we call an act "immoral," we prescind from all partisan and parochial perspectives and think we are talking the universal human language, the language of reason, and consequently can rightfully expect all rational persons to agree with us.

Since the debate over the life-death issues and the new biology takes place in the public forum, and since many of the participants in the debate are non-believers, one does not hear much talk of "sin" except from the fundamentalist factions. The discourse is framed more in terms of "moral evil" than "sin." This in no way puts Catholic participants at a disadvantage, since the Catholic tradition is equally rich and wise in either framework. What it does do, however, and equally for all participants in the dialogue be they theists or atheists, is require that arguments be based not on any religious authority, but be couched in strictly rational terms. It simply being assumed that the "rational" thing is always the "moral" thing as well. (We shall have occasion to speak to this assumption a bit later.)

When it comes to morality, there have always been two easily identifiable approaches, which are captured rather nicely in a story told by Andre Siegfried, a French writer. It seems an English friend of his once heard a French mother admonish her little boy of three years with the words: "Sois raisonnable!" (Be reasonable!). The Englishman was amazed at this expression, because he remembered his own mother having said to him on similar occasions: "Be a good boy!" Siegfried and his English friend both agreed that "Be a good boy!" really meant "Do what you are told!," while "Be reasonable!" did not have that connotation. At least not in the first place.

We have in this story the two main strands of the common opinion about moral questions. One opinion says that the heart of the matter is a set of obligations, duties, moral laws and imperatives which must be obeyed. The other sees the central issue to be an end to be striven for, a moral order to be established, a reasonableness to be lived up to. Now the task of reason is to discern, make and establish a right order in things; that is always its primary work. In the first case, the ideal of a truly human life is seen as obedience to laws; while in the second it is seen as conformity to reason.

More often than not there will be nothing to choose between these two approaches when it comes to deciding more obvious moral issues, because the proponents of each position will happily agree. But even when they agree, which is not always the case, there is a very significant difference between the two positions. For in the former the order has been established in advance by the law-giver, and there is really nothing left for humankind to do, but to obey or disobey. In the latter, it is the task of reason, i.e. of humankind, to establish the right moral order precisely because that moral order cannot be fully known in advance. There is a human grandeur and nobility of vocation in the latter approach which is totally lacking in the former, which calls only for total submission and obedience.

Now the Catholic tradition in morality is equally at home in either approach. This leads to some ambiguity and confusion in the minds of the faithful as they see the church sometimes invoking obedience to Divine Law as the reason for its position, and at other times having recourse to right order which is the primary work of reason. On many issues both approaches reach the same conclusion, but as new moral dilemmas are created by advances in science and technology, we are faced with situations not covered explicitly by Divine Law, so the reasoned approach becomes central. This is certainly true with regard to the life-death issues which are currently the central focus of so much moral investigation and reasoning.

Of course, the problem is that when one presents a moral argument or position from the perspective of human reason, one may find that other reasoned positions claim equal validity, and so disputes and disagreements between persons of obvious good will come to mark the enterprise. That is the predicament contemporary Catholics find themselves in with regard to the current discussion of the morality of the new life-death technologies. And having entered the debate in the open forum where public reason prevails, recourse to Divine or ecclesial authority is not only ineffective, it is judged to be inappropriate.

Fortunately, the Catholic tradition on morals is not one dimensional, relying solely on Divine Revelation, Scripture or the arguments from faith. In addition to those sorts of arguments, it has always had a strong tradition of philosophical moral arguments, based on the ontological nature of human beings, their lives and their actions. It has come to be known as a "natural law" ethic, but that is an unfortunate appellation for two reasons. First, it makes the Catholic church appear to be legalistic in both its perspectives (faith and reason) on morals. And second, it does not do real justice to the Catholic philosophical tradition and the creative role of reason by suggesting that obedience to the law is really what is called for. Be that as it may, in the current controversies with non-believers over the morality of the new medical technologies, the church makes effective use of its so-called natural law tradition. With believers, of course, it is able to invoke not only reason and natural law, but Divine Law and the Lord's dream of the Kingdom as well.

1. *The Starting Point*

Unlike so many contemporary moral theories, the Catholic tradition in ethics does not consider morality to be primarily a matter of rights but a matter of right. One does not determine the morality of an act by seeking to know whose rights were violated, but rather by determining on some ontological basis what *is* right. It will not do, therefore, to suggest that women have a "right" to an abortion, unless one has first determined that abortion is right. The Catholic tradition maintains, I think quite correctly, the priority of right over rights. One can only have a right to something on the condition that that something *is* right. So moral inquiry and discourse begin with determining what is right and why, not with determining who has rights and what are their limits.

Like all starting points, this one rests on a basic assumption. The assumption that the universe is not absurd but an ordered whole and that it, therefore, makes eminent sense for rational persons to try to determine what is morally right. Put another way, were we, as rational beings, unable to infer what we *ought* to do and become from the way it is with us and our world, then moral striving and moral dialogue would not only be meaningless, they would be impossible.[2] So, the very fact that we human beings are rational; that there exists deep within us the drive to question and the search for meaning; that we are capable of recognizing immorality and identifying a moral issue; that we know when the ways things *are* is not the way they *ought* to be—all indicate that life is not meaningless or absurd, and that there is, or ought to be, a rational order to human life. At least that is the basic starting point for traditional Catholic ethics.

2. *Combating Ethical Relativism*

As the Catholic moral tradition never tires of pointing out, without some such starting point, morality is reduced to conventionally agreed upon codes of conduct which are relative to one's culture, to the age in which one lives, to one's race or gender and to the so-called advances in science and technology. There are no objective, hard and fast, moral rules which transcend the particularities of culture, of one's age, race or gender, and which are universally true.

The Catholic moral tradition rightly abhors such ethical relativism, and has been consistent in always fighting against it. This has become a very significant factor in our day. Not only does the Catholic tradition speak out against the obvious moral relativism of the non-believers of our day, it actually accuses anyone who wants to revise the traditional view in any way of having fallen into ethical relativism.[3] It is the harshest judgment that can rendered about a Catholic moral theory, because no true believer wants anything to do with ethical relativism. It is obviously inimical to the faith.

Ethical relativism is the view that ethical truths are all relative, which means that the rightness or wrongness of an action and the goodness of an object depend on or consist in the attitude taken toward them by some individual or group, and hence may vary from individual to individual or from group to group. It is perhaps an indication of the tenor of our times that such arbitrariness in moral matters is not only *not* viewed as a rather bizarre position to adopt, but has actually become a taken-for-granted assumption for a significant number of eminent moral philosophers.

By no means of recent origin, ethical relativism dates back to the first beginnings of Western philosophy, and is particularly associated with the Sophist, Protagoras of Abdera (490-421 B.C.). Protagoras maintained that in the perception of sense qualities, as well as of the moral and aesthetic qualities of reality, the individual "man is the measure of all things." This doctrine was so effectively countered by Plato, in his dialogues the *Theaetetus* and the *Protagoras,* and by Aristotle and others, that while ethical relativism always remained psychologically attractive to human beings, it was never seen as having any real legitimate metaphysical or logical foundation. It remained in the ancient world, at best, a minority opinion. The advent of Christianity put objective Western morality on a supernatural and theological foundation, further lowering the credibility of ethical relativism. So it was that for centuries the metaphysical and religious tradition of the West prevented relativism from becoming a potent factor in moral theory or ethics, but it always lurked in the wings awaiting its chance to get on stage, never dreaming that the 20th century would see it come to occupy center stage in one form or another.

The resurgence of ethical relativism has been due to many factors, but, speaking generally, the movement away from any metaphysics and away from religion and theology has done away with the objective natural foundation for morality which had for so long characterized Western thought. In those circumstances, it was inevitable that ethical relativism would gain in respectability. But for it to have become the "new tradition" and to have moved to center stage, is due to certain very specific factors.

As far back as 1955, Abraham Edel[4] identified several important strands in the fabric of contemporary relativism. First, there is the growing view that morality is not based on any divine foundation, be it divine commands or natural law, that it is entirely a product of human making. If one accepts a Darwinian view of human evolution, then morality too must have evolved along with the race. Religion, far from offering morality a firm objective foundation, is itself a product of human evolution just as morality is. For many then, morality and religion are just two more human products ''fashioned by man in his collective effort to make his home on the face of the globe.''

The modern age is marked by the rise of individualistic egoism. Each person is seen to be the ultimate judge of her own case. Thanks to egoistic philosophies such as those of Hobbes, Bentham, Freud and Sartre, it is now taken for granted that there are ''no social obligations not subject to individual veto.'' It is every man and every woman for his or her self. Whatever restrictions on personal behavior the individual accepts, she does so in behalf of her own longer term self-interest. Morality is viewed in utilitarian terms, becoming no more than a means of insuring the greatest good for the greatest number. An impossible task when there is no common agreement on what is good.

Then there is the mechanistic view of the human person prevalent today in both psychology and education. As Pavlov conditioned his dogs, and Skinner his pigeons, so too human beings are conditioned in their behavior. Whether this conditioning is done scientifically or allowed to happen haphazardly, many feel that we are totally determined in the ways we think and act by the milieu or environment in which we live. Given that assessment of the human condition, morality is no longer a viable enterprise, since one must be free to be held morally responsible. Also, if we are totally conditioned by our culture to behave in the way that we do, then obviously, since there are different cultures, there will be a wide variety of behavior patterns and values on which human beings base their conduct, and absolutely no way to decide between them other than personal or cultural preference. Ethical relativity once again.

No one of these factors could by itself have resurrected relativism to legitimate status, but the convergence of them all has contributed to the vitality of that position in our day. Commenting on the effect of that convergence, Edel remarks:

> There can be no doubt as to the convergent effect. The design that is formed is one of arbitrariness in ethics. This is the focus of much popular and philosophical thinking on the question. For human values, human goals, human aspirations come to appear as products of self-seeking, of cultural indoctrination, . . . of man's mere animal nature. If morality is man-made and if it is changing, there is no purpose metaphysically or theologically imposed. If egoism is correct, there are no morally mandatory social obligations not subject to individual veto. . . . If the mind is a clean slate or the body an almost wholly plastic material, then almost anything is possible. If cultural relativity is a sociological truth, then your morality is a function of your domicile. If moral assertions are simply expressive, it all depends on how you feel. In any case, it all depends . . . [5]

And in a spirit of levity which belies the seriousness of this situation, Edel sums it all up in a little jingle:

> It all depends on where you are,
> It all depends on when you are,
> It all depends on what you feel,
> It all depends on how you feel,

It all depends on how you're raised,
It all depends on what is praised,
What's right today is wrong tomorrow,
Joy in France, in England sorrow.
It all depends on point of view,
Australia or Timbuctoo,
In Rome do as the Romans do,
If tastes just happen to agree
Then you have morality.
But where there are conflicting trends,
It all depends, it all depends...[6]

No matter how often I rehearse this account of the resurgence of ethical relativism to myself, I just cannot help being utterly amazed that there are people, much less philosophers, who actually take it seriously. Say there is no God, say that metaphysics is all poetry, though I may disagree with you, I won't question your rationality. But try to convince me of the absolute relativity of moral values, and I shall have trouble vouching for your sanity. I make no claim of being able to justify that reaction, I just want to admit that it is there.

When I question myself about it, I am forced to face the objection that the reason I feel that way is because I was myself formed intellectually within both a metaphysical and a religious tradition. I have been unable to convince myself that that is all there is to it. And the residue left after bracketing out those factors, seems to me to be something which Daniel Maguire calls "to know believingly." Concerning that sort of knowing he wrote:

> Believing is *knowing* what you cannot see or prove, but what you still accept and hold with firmness. Life is full of such faith-knowl-

> edge, a kind of knowledge that has its source in affectivity. Every lover knows this. The lover cannot explain or justify with reasons the insights of his heart. And yet he calmly believes that those make consummate sense. . . . But it is not knowledge of the sort that basks in self-evidence. What we accept on faith might even seem on its face absurd. And yet it appears even more absurd not to believe. We "hang in there" with what we believe because the alternative is unbearable and we could make no sense of it.[7]

It is the existence of this sort of knowledge in human life which continues to offer experiential support to some sort of objectively based morality.

To my mind, then, ethical relativism is absurd on the face of it, I can make no sense of it, it is an unbearable alternative which makes ethics irrelevant, and common life impossible. It is simply not to be believed. If every moral value is relative and none universal, then we cannot condemn slavery, child abuse, murder, rape and sexism, categorically. The most we can say is that we would prefer to not see such things in our culture. I find that completely counter-intuitive and totally irrational. Still, ethical relativism remains the prevailing popular view, which profoundly affects the current discussions about the morality of the new life-death technologies. And as has always been the case, the Catholic church wisely brings to the current public dialogue an abhorrence of ethical relativism and a commitment to the natural order of things under God.

3. *Determining The Morality of An Act*

Non-Catholics have trouble understanding the Catholic moral position because they think that the morality of an act is determined by whether or not the act causes harm. The prevailing view is that the morality of an act is determined solely by its consequences. No harm done, then no immorality either. Viewed that way, acts such as masturbation and birth control are clearly not immoral. But traditional Catholic morality is not that simplistic, being sensitive to many other factors which affect the morality of an act in addition to its consequences. That judging the morality of an act simply from its consequences is not sufficient can be clearly seen if one but reflects on two everyday sorts of situations.

Suppose one intends to do real harm to another person, just for the sake of the pleasure one takes in such activity. One makes plans to do so, and is prevented from carrying out the plan by unexpected circumstances. No harm is done, yet one senses that there is something immoral about the situation nonetheless. Or suppose that one intends to grace one's neighbor with a great good, but as things turn out, again due to circumstances beyond our control, great harm is inadvertently done instead. Though our action caused unforeseen and unwilled harm, though it consequences were harmful, who would say that we had acted immorally? Clearly, judging the morality of our actions is a much more complex enterprise than simply adding up the pluses and minuses in terms of consequences.

In a word, according to the Catholic tradition, human acts are multi-layered, like onions, and in order for our acts to be morally good, they must display the proper rectitude (or right order) not only in their consequences, but in all of their many layers. If one element of our action is disordered, that disorder, like a cancer, affects the whole act; so only an action which manifests right order throughout can be judged to be integrally good and moral. Sometimes the disorder is minimal or peripheral, lessening the moral goodness of an act but not destroying it. At other times, the disorder is at the heart of the act, making the act immoral in its very nature. But whatever the case, in the Catholic tradition judging the morality of an act is more than just assessing whether it has good or bad results, it also requires a discernment of whether those results were achieved in the right way, that is, in accord with the right order required by the nature of things, the nature of human persons and of human actions.

It is only if one understands that "rectitude" and not "consequences" are at the heart of traditional Catholic moral theory, that one can find the meaning in the church's moral counsel on such things as birth control and masturbation. Given the nature of things, such acts are disordered. We are at liberty to do them anyway, of course, but our freedom does not extend to changing the natural order of things. That is beyond our competence. No matter how much we could wish things were otherwise, things are what they are. Freedom's task is not to determine what constitutes right order and what does not, i.e. what is moral and what is immoral, that has been taken care of by God, the author of nature. Freedom's primary moral task is to choose to live in accord with right order or not.

While this approach makes the Catholic church look old fashioned and intransigent in moral matters to many, to others the Catholic church is a sign of consistency and sanity in an otherwise insane world. Though predictable, the Catholic church can always be counted on to speak in favor of the right natural order of things. For it to do otherwise, would be for it to break with its venerable moral tradition.

4. *The Relevant Moral Rectitudes of the Human Act*

For an act even to be subject to moral evaluation by oneself or by others, it must be voluntary and the result of conscious choice. Only then is it a truly "human act" capable of taking on the character of being either "moral" or "immoral." The very fact that a human act involves choice, leads one to immediately ask two questions. "What" is it that the agent chose to do in this act and "why" did she choose it? The tradition speaks of the "what" as the *object of the act,* and of the "why" as the *end of the agent.* In determining the essential morality of any freely chosen action, one must ascertain whether there is a disorder, lack of rectitude, in either the *object* or the *end.* A disorder in either vitiates the act, making it basically immoral.

But the *end* has primacy over the object, because the act which is performed is always related to the end as the chosen way of achieving it, i.e. as a means to the end. So the question of the rectitude of the means becomes a moot point, if the *end,* or intention of the agent, is already skewered and disordered. If one originates an act with the direct intention of doing evil, the act is immoral regardless of the means used to achieve it.

Interest in the rectitude of the *object* as the means to the intended end arises only on condition that the end sought is not a disordered one. In the rather uncomplicated cases of masturbation and birth control (contraception), the disorder in the object is so apparent that no reason (end), however good and properly ordered, can redeem the act from its inherent immorality. In each of those cases, the agent uses his or her sexual powers in a way which is *contra naturam,* contrary to the procreative nature of human sexuality. But to choose to achieve some end by means of an act which is inherently disordered is precisely what the Catholic tradition means when it labels an act immoral because a good end *never* justifies an evil means.

But even should the rectitude of end and object be established, the process of moral discernment is not yet complete. For a good end, achieved by an act which is properly ordered, may still be performed in situations and circumstances which could skewer the right order of the act taken in its totality. A non-contraceptive act of intercourse between spouses in order to express their love for one another is an act which is properly ordered with respect to both the *object* and the *end.* But were such an act to be a part of a public pornographic display which incited others to lust, those circumstances would alter the moral character of the act.

So it is that the Catholic tradition insists on avoiding a one-dimensional assessment of the morality of human acts. To judge the morality of human actions, one must look to the intention of the agent, to the intrinsic nature of the act itself, and to any circumstances which might alter the moral character of the act in question. Thus it is that the tradition declares the morality of an act to be determined by the END, OBJECT and CIRCUMSTANCES of that act.[8] If the end does not violate the natural order of things, then one must look to the object as a possible source of immorality. If the end and the object do not violate right order, then one must still look to the circumstances before judging the act to be a moral one. Those of our acts which have the proper rectitude in all three, are most fully and integrally morally good acts.

5. *Reason and Natural Law*

Since rectitude or right order is central to morality, and since order is always understood to be the result of intelligence not chaos, it is not surprising that the Catholic moral tradition puts so much stock in human reason. The connection between morality (moral rectitude) and human reason is so intimate that reason is a condition for and a pre-requisite to morality. So much so, that at times the tradition speaks of "right reason" *(recta ratio)* as the ultimate natural norm of morality.

But reason's relationship to right order is twofold. It is by means of our reasoning power that we are able to discover and discern the natural order of things. And once having done that, it is through reason that we are able to create order in our thought, and in our lives. Thomas Aquinas thought that the various kinds of sciences could actually be distinguished on the basis of their relationship to order. In the prologue to his commentary on the *Ethics* of Aristotle, he wrote:

> As Aristotle says in the beginning of the *Metaphysics* (Bk. I, chp. 2), it is the business of the wise man to order. The reason for this is that wisdom is the most powerful perfection of reason whose characteristic is to *know order.* Even if the sense powers know some things in themselves, nevertheless *to know the order of one thing to another is exclusively the work of intellect or reason.*

He then continues:

> Now order is related to reason in a fourfold way. There is *first* an order that reason does not establish but only beholds, such is the order of things in nature. It is the function of the natural sciences to consider the order of things that human reason considers but does not establish... There is a *second* order that reason establishes in its own act of intellection, this order that reason makes in its own intellectual acts is the work of logic... There is a *third* order that reason in deliberating establishes in the operations of the will. *This order of voluntary actions pertains to the consideration of moral philosophy or ethics.* There is a fourth order that reason in planning establishes in the external things which it causes, such as a chest or a house. This order which reason establishes in the external things of the world arranged by human reason pertains to the mechanical arts...
>
> Accordingly it is proper to moral philosophy, to which our attention is at present directed, to consider human operations insofar as they are ordered to one another and to an end. I am talking about "human" operations, those springing from man's will following the order of reason.[9]

We see captured here the heart of the Catholic moral tradition. Endowed with reason and the capacity for wisdom, human beings are able to know things not only in their isolated individuality, but also as Aquinas noted, to know "the order of one thing to another." This specifically "human" ability changes absolutely everything for us. It constitutes us as moral agents, which means that we are not able, like the animals, to simply live, simply seek pleasure, and simply die. Reason makes us conscious of a moral order which calls for our response, one way or the other. As moral agents we not only can know what is required of us if we would be true to the God-given order of things, but we can also discern disorder whenever it occurs, in our own acts and in those of others. More than that, as free moral agents we are also capable of being the *originators of disorder,* of being, in a word, immoral.

Immorality begins by a freely introduced disorder into our very selves, into our very wills. But as everyone knows, it does not end there. Because we are naturally "ordered" to one another, actions which proceed from a disordered will, a will unwilling to accept the right order which reason has discerned, affect others. Sometimes with devastating results. When we act as if we were the only ones on the planet, when our desires and interests are sought without thought for the effect on others, when we act as if there were no limits to what we can do, our actions lack the proper rectitude even before we examine their consequences, i.e. the harm done. Acting mindless of right order or against it, is precisely what the Catholic tradition means by saying we violate the *natural law.*

Natural law is simply the "right order" of things human. To act against the natural law is to violate the proper relationship which should obtain between human beings and their world, and between human persons and one another. Some elements of that "right order," and therefore some parts of natural law, are so elementary and evident that they have been incorporated into the mores of every culture, every society. Murder, stealing, lying are obvious examples. Common life is threatened to the core by these things, and so every society interdicts them. But the right order of other things, especially those made possible by the new biological technologies, is not so simply discerned. Can the Catholic moral tradition make an important contribution to the current discussions about those things? What contribution can it make to the dialogue about life-death issues in our day?

Before answering those questions, it should be recalled, as already noted, that the Catholic moral tradition is currently being challenged from within the household of the faith by those I have called "revisionists." There is not unanimity within the Catholic church about the meaning and application of its moral tradition to the moral issues of our day. Without in any way denigrating the tremendous contribution of that tradition to the human race over the centuries, some Catholics are beginning to question it on some crucial points. So before turning to the application of Catholic morality to the life-death issues of our time, it would, perhaps, be wise to consider a more contemporary Catholic interpretation of morality. To that, we now turn.

NOTES TO CHAPTER II

1. On the distinction between "moral evil" and "sin," and why every moral evil is a sin, but not every sin a moral evil, see: Dick Westley, *Morality And Its Beyond,* Twenty-Third Publications, Mystic, CT, 2nd Printing, 1985, Chp. 2, "The Origin of Evil And The Need For Morality," pp. 29-46.

2. Most contemporary moralists agree with David Hume (1711-1776) that there can be no *ought* derived from is, now known as Hume's Law. (Cf. David Hume, *Treatise On Human Nature,* Bk. III, Pt. 1, Section 1.) What Hume's law effectively does is cut the connection between the world of fact and the world of value, and it does so so completely that the consequence is that ethical values have no grounding whatsoever in reality.

This opens the door to the contemporary malaise of ethical relativism, where there are no objective moral standards, but moral positions are merely a matter of personal preference and hence may vary from individual to individual, from culture to culture. (On that point, see: Allan Bloom, *The Closing Of The American Mind,* Simon & Schuster, New York, 1987.) Catholic ethics, having been conceived and fashioned long before the advent of Hume's Law, has been generally unaffected by it, and continues to offer to the world a wise alternative to ethical relativism.

3. In the current discussions going on between moral theologians, the accusation of the traditionalists against the revisionists is that they have adopted a purely utilitarian ethic, by which the traditionalists mean to say that they have succumbed to ethical relativism. In the next chapter we shall see something of the revisionist position, and the reader will be able to judge for herself whether the traditionalist accusations are correct.

4. Abraham Edel, *Ethical Judgment,* Free Press, 1955, pp. 19-27.

5. *Ibid.*, pp. 27-28.

6. *Ibid.*, p. 16.

7. Daniel Maguire, *Moral Choice,* Doubleday, 1978, pp. 87-88.

8. Thomas Aquinas, *Summa Theologiae,* I-II, Q.18-20.

9. Thomas Aquinas, *Commentary on the Nicomachean Ethics of Aristotle,* Regnery, Chicago, 1964.

CHAPTER THREE
Calls For Revision

IT is always possible to interpret any call for revision in the Catholic moral tradition as arising from a desire to be free of the limiting constraints of the traditional position. That is to say, from a succumbing to current hedonistic values and moral laxism. Certainly one must always be on guard against such things. They are not "moral" positions at all, but are rather the rejection of moral obligation in favor of naked self-interest. Nothing more need be said about them. But perhaps there is something to be said for a moral position which rejects both the cultural drift toward hedonism, as well as the traditional Catholic understanding of moral rectitude and natural law.

1. *The Contemporary Challenges to Catholic Morality*

The first challenge comes from contemporary philosophy, especially from contemporary European philosophy.[1] Its phenomenological study of the human person and her freedom raises a serious challenge to the traditional Catholic perspective on morality. What makes the challenge a serious and well intentioned one, is the fact that it suggests that the traditional view of human freedom is inadequate. Consequently, any moral theory based on that inadequate view is bound to be flawed.

In general, three things characterize the movement of contemporary European philosophy, no matter what differences there may be between the philosophers taken individually. They all share a common concern, employ a common method, and generally agree on a common set of basic insights.

Their common concern is humankind, they seek no more nor less than the meaning of human life. For what can we realistically hope in this life? What can we accomplish, and what is the goal and meaning of our mysterious freedom? Their philosophy, then, is a philosophy of the human. God may, or may not, enter into their considerations.

Their method is phenomenological, that is to say they eschew empty abstractions and reflectively spell out the significance of their personal encounters with the world. What does human experience reveal about the meaning of human life and the human vocation?

Of their common insights, two in particular challenge the traditional Catholic view of morality. For growing numbers of contemporary philosophers, human existence is marked by an indelible contingency. Reality is experienced as having a malleability, a moldability and a pliability which makes us ever aware that however things are, they could always be otherwise. Nothing is fated, history is no mere unfolding of a pre-established order. And secondly, as a correlate of reality's plasticity, the shape of things is humankind's major responsibility. The task of human reason is not seen as the acceptance of a pre-established order, but rather the imaginative improvement of it. We are here not to passively accept what is given, but to change it for the better. That is the human vocation. That is what it means to be human.

Our freedom, then, is *not* to be reduced to the power to choose or not to choose to conform to the pre-established order. It is precisely because human beings are free that they exist in a plastic world awaiting their input and imprint. It would be contradictory for us to live in a world where everything was predetermined. In such a world, human freedom could have no meaning. Our freedom is a freedom to create, to invent order without the benefit of pre-established plans. The moral goodness of human acts cannot be the result of mere conformity to fixed structures or natures, if for no other reason than because there are none. These philosophers call for the guidelines of human conduct to be shifted from fixed natures to open ideals, from rigid pre-established patterns to inventive creativity, from passive conformity to imaginative ingenuity.

Thus it is that the contribution of contemporary philosophy is its insight into the work and vocation of being human, of human freedom and intelligence. The meaning of existence is not so fully fashioned that all we can do is to either ratify or reject it. That is an impoverished view of human freedom. Rather, as creative sources of intelligibility and value, we are autonomous sources charged with and responsible for making sense of our world.

a. *The Challenge of Atheism*[2]

Two significant atheistic Continental (European) philosophers from whom believers can learn much on this issue, are Karl Marx and Jean Paul Sartre. Whatever else we may have against these thinkers, each is a champion of human freedom and responsibility.

It was the stifling of human responsibility, and of our creative role in life, which Karl Marx deplored in the economic conditions of his day. The economic and political repression of the 19th century destroyed human autonomy and left us little more than our biological existence. For Marx, the call of religion, and therefore of the Catholic moral tradition as well, to submit to a pre-established natural order in the hope of liberation and freedom in the afterlife, were just additional means of repressing human autonomy. The lasting power of the revolution which Marx heralded, despite its other shortcomings, was his insistence that human beings take responsibility for their world, something which the post-Vatican II Catholic church is also urging now in matters of economic justice and peace. If anything characterizes Marx's vision, it is his call for us to employ our human ingenuity and freedom not to accept the world as it is, but to imaginatively improve it.

It is that same vision which animates the thought of French existentialist Jean Paul Sartre. During World War II, a young student came to Sartre torn between remaining in France under the occupation as the sole support of his mother, or risking his life with the French resistance in Algeria. He asked Sartre which was the better course of action. Sartre gave the lad the rather distressing counsel that because there was no better or best choice prior to a person's choosing, that the young man would have to "invent" or "create" the choice which would be better or best. That was his responsibility. No one could do it for him, and no one could advise him prior to his own lonely decision. No one, Sartre thought, not priest, professor or counselor could say before the fact of a responsible choice which course of action would be better or best in a given situation. For Sartre, there can be no prior claims on freedom's response. Human freedom is always creative, else it isn't freedom but a counterfeit.

It is this commitment to the creativity of freedom which led Sartre to his atheism. Some feel that he was not so much rejecting God, as the traditional picture of God put forth by Christianity. He is attacking not God, nor faith in God, but every form of theological thinking which attempts to rob human beings of their freedom in favor of an illusion which transforms our existence into a fixed or pre- established destiny (predestination). If morality is conformity to a pre-established order, the dignity and grandeur of human beings capable of creating moral order is eschewed. We can make not real contributions to morality, because literally there is nothing left for us to do. Thus, we are robbed of our very life, that is of our creative responsibility for the world, and of our capacity for autonomous self direction.

Now it is no accident that Marx and Sartre both couple their affirmation of humankind's creative responsibility for the world with a militant atheism, a militant anti-Christianity. For what kind of a God would give us reason, imagination, freedom, and the desire to create order and then call on us to simply conform to a pre-established order? If things are as the tradition says they are, these two philosophers see no alternative but to deny the existence of God, for the God whom they see Christianity presenting is a contradiction. Such a God can no more exist or be conceived than can a square circle.

What rings true in the image of the human person which contemporary philosophy, and Marx and Sartre in particular, give, is their rejection of all forms of thinking which reduce human existence to conformity to fixed, pre-established, patterns. Under the challenge of people like Marx and Sartre, believers must re-think their cherished traditional ways of regarding morality. We must re-think the position which says that our role in life is simply to find the order which God has established and conform to it. That is to view human beings impersonally, almost mechanically. Contemporary philosophy wisely counsels believers to abandon impersonal categories when thinking about morality and God's dealings with us, and to make room for the grandeur of the human, i.e. creative responsibility not only for the world but for the morality of human life as well.

b. *The Challenge From Within: Revisionism*

While it is true that we live in a culture and a time greatly influenced by both Marx and Sartre, not all the challenges to the Catholic moral tradition come from outside the household of the faith. As noted earlier, there is currently a strong challenge being brought forth in the name of Thomas Aquinas by moral theologians whom Rome calls "proportionalists," and whom I prefer to call the "revisionists."[3]

Their challenge to the seeming rigidity of the traditional Catholic moral tradition does not center around the meaning of human freedom and our responsibility for the world, as did the challenge of Marx and Sartre. They seem to have a much more modest disagreement with the tradition. They are concerned to correct and revise the traditional interpretation of Thomas Aquinas as a thinker who held that acts can be intrinsically evil. That is to say, that there are acts which are in and of themselves morally evil, and that when such acts are made the "object" of choice, the subsequent action cannot but be immoral. This, at first, seems like a very small revision indeed, but actually it constitutes the major internal challenge to traditional Catholic morality, as Rome well understands.

Whatever else one may know about the Catholic church, everyone knows that such acts as blasphemy, masturbation, contraceptive love-making between spouses, pre- and extra-marital sex, murder and abortion are all intrinsically evil acts, and are always prohibited. The fact that there may be mitigating subjective conditions lessening the guilt of the perpetrator of such acts, the acts *in themselves* are always morally evil. Thus while the personal culpability of such acts may be affected by the situational context in which they were done, no circumstance, no situation, in fact nothing, can lessen their intrinsically evil character, since they are *by nature* morally evil. About that the tradition has no doubts whatsoever.

Enter the revisionists. It had been customary to read St. Thomas Aquinas as saying exactly what the tradition says. Indeed, as *the* major Catholic moral thinker, his influence on the tradition has been enormous. The current revisionist moral theologians have made a compelling case that Aquinas did not really uphold the tradition on the matter of the intrinsic goodness or badness of actions in themselves. Following the lead of Dom Lottin[4], who thirty years ago showed that Aquinas did indeed repeat the traditional view in many texts, but never in his own name and always as being the traditional position of his own day, they have presumed to present Aquinas' true position. If the revisionists are correct in their reinterpretation of Aquinas, then not only does that make Aquinas a more revolutionary moral thinker than was supposed, it also challenges in our own day the validity of the way the Catholic church continues to speak about certain acts as intrinsically evil. The battle is joined.

The Historical Battle Over Intrinsic Morality

Our problem was explicitly posed by Peter Abelard in his *Ethica* (circa 1135), where he asks whether human acts are of their nature morally indifferent, or whether there are certain acts which because of their object, independently of any subjective element from the agent, are intrinsically good or intrinsically evil. Ironically, due to the revisionist challenge this medieval problem is now the burning moral issue within the church as well. Some problems seem never to go away, but reappear throughout history.

In the Catholic tradition a human act is divided into the interior act and the exterior act. The interior act is an act of the will and involves the intention of the agent or end for which she acts. The exterior act is the action performed to carry out the agent's intention and to achieve her end. Now for Abelard, the exterior act is morally indifferent, for example the act of killing someone. By saying that such an act is morally indifferent, Abelard does not mean that it makes no difference whether one kills another or not. Rather, he means that the act of killing is morally indifferent until one factors in the intention of the agent. Or to put it another way, a morally indifferent act can be in the concrete either morally good or morally evil. Which it is, depends on the intention of the agent. If I am killing in self-defense, or if I am carrying out a lawful execution the action is morally good. If, on the other hand, I am seeking revenge or engaging in wanton cruelty for pleasure, then obviously the acts are morally evil.

For Abelard, then, everything depends on what the agent has in mind as she acts. It would be hard to conceive a more explicit rejection of the intrinsic morality of acts. What Abelard was straining to express was that part of the Catholic tradition which has always held that morality is not a matter of external observances, but of the heart and will.

On the other side of the issue was Peter Lombard (d. 1160). He thought that certain acts were so intrinsically evil, in and of themselves, that no intention, however good, could alter their intrinsic malice. He thought that Abelard's point about intention was valid only when applied to intrinsically good acts which could be made evil by a bad intention, not to intrinsically evil ones. Such acts are morally evil in themselves prior to any consideration of the will and intention of the agent. Therefore, no intention or good end could ever be used to justify such actions. Lombard's way of talking about the morality of human acts became the traditional frame of reference for the later Middle Ages, and hence was the prevailing context within which Thomas Aquinas worked and thought. In that context, the act taken in itself without reference to the agent was called the OBJECT, and the intention of the agent was either said to be a CIRCUMSTANCE of the act (object) or by later thinkers the END of the agent. And as we have already seen, the Catholic tradition has thereafter insisted on judging the morality of a human act by looking at all three, on the assumption that each can be either morally good or evil and must be looked at in themselves.

The revisionists of our day have given Aquinas' views on the matter a very close reading and a very thorough analysis, and claim to have discovered that even though he reports the traditional view correctly, he departs from it when speaking in his own name. In a word, it now seems to be fairly well established that Aquinas is much closer to Abelard than to Lombard and the tradition.[5]

Evidently, Aquinas fears that judging the moral goodness or evil of an act by discerning the goodness of the object, end and circumstances overlooks the fact that in reality there is only one act. However, many elements go to make up a human act, i.e. one subject to moral judgment, *in the moral order they all coalesce to form a single, unique and indivisible act.* He writes: "It is important to note that the interior act of the will and the external action, *when they are considered in the "moral" order, are one act.*" He then goes on to say:

> . . . So we must say that when the external action derives goodness or malice exclusively from its relation to the end alone, then obviously there is only one goodness of the act of the will and of the external action. But when an external action has some measure of goodness in itself, because of fitting matter and proper circumstances, then that goodness is distinct from the goodness of the will according to the end. Still, even in that case we would say that the goodness of the end passes over to the external action, and the goodness of the fitting matter and proper circumstances passes over into the act of the will (*Summa Theologiae* I-II, 20,).

The tradition seems to want to add up the "goodnesses" of the object, end and circumstances in such a way that it assumes that there is a "moral" goodness of the object, a "moral" goodness of the end (or intention)," and a "moral" goodness of the circumstances, and that for an act to be morally acceptable each of these three elements must be "morally" good. How else to understand the assertion that there are some acts (objects) which are intrinsically immoral? There can be no doubt that that is how the Catholic moral teaching is usually presented to people, even if there are sophisticated theoretical distinctions invoked by expert moralists to better safeguard the unity of moral acts. In order to understand Aquinas, so the revisionists tell us, one has to take a different perspective altogether and almost speak a different moral language.

Aquinas' Contribution To the Current Debate[6]

We have become so accustomed to identifying Aquinas with the tradition that it may prove difficult for us to be open to an alternative, revisionist, interpretation. The fact is that the textbook accounts of Aquinas are generally not nuanced enough to do him justice. So perhaps we have to put aside our preconceptions, and attempt to "hear" Aquinas with new ears. To help with that, let me cite the seldom quoted lines from his prologue to the second part of the *Summa Theologiae.* As the very first words of his most important moral treatise they are instructive and illuminating. One has to do no more than read them to understand why they are rarely quoted:

> The subject matter to be considered in this part is man, inasmuch as he is God's image, which is to say: Inasmuch as he, like God, is the principle of his own actions, having the power of free choice and the authority to govern himself (Prologue, *Summa Theologiae* I-II).[7]

Clearly, Aquinas would well understand the efforts of the atheists, Marx and Sartre, to affirm human responsibility for the world. And lest one think that this is making too much of a single sentence from Aquinas, it is good to recall that Aquinas championed the grandeur of humankind long before Marx and Sartre. Speaking of divine providence, Aquinas wrote:

> All things are subject to divine providence, but rational creatures are so in a superior way. For they are under divine providence by participating in it, for they are called in some way to be divine providence for themselves and for others (*Summa Theologiae* I-II, 91, 2, c).

The point to be noted here is that when we find the revised Aquinas talking against the intrinsic moral nature of acts (the object), this is not out of character for him at all. Indeed, in the two statements just cited, he gives a clear indication of what his overview of morality is going to be, and so we should not be surprised to find him parting company with the tradition on that issue. Were he to have simply repeated the traditional account, he would have gone back on what he said in the Prologue, and would have undercut his commitment to the grandeur of humankind. Recognizing that should be reason enough to give the revisionist claim about him an unbiased hearing.

In the simplest terms, Aquinas thinks that the moral designations "good" and "evil" apply fundamentally, primarily and essentially to acts of the will. The will is morally good, if what it intends, the end (the will's object, not "object" as the tradition speaks of it, i.e. as the act in and of itself) is morally good.[8] And the intention or end of the agent is good only if it is measured and proportioned to right reason *(recta ratio)*.[9]

Thus far, Aquinas pretty much agrees with the tradition. But when he comes to discuss the external act, his originality begins to move him away from that tradition. As we have already noted, Aquinas thinks of the human act as an integral whole, much the same way that he thinks of the human person composed of body and soul. Though it is important to make the distinction between the internal act of the will, and the external act commanded by the will to achieve its chosen end, those two parts of the human act cannot be viewed as physical parts which are joined accidentally simply by being juxtaposed to each other. Such an incidental linking of parts would ruin the ontological integrity of the human act, and make its moral character, be it good or evil, completely circumstantial.

For Aquinas, the internal and external aspects of a voluntary human act must interpenetrate each other, much the way soul and body do in the living person, yielding a single act with a single moral character of value. In the jargon of his day, he speaks of them as related as matter and form. Now in all such matter-form relationships, the composite gets its nature from its form. It is the formal element which confers on a thing its specificity. With regard to morality and the human act, that specificity comes from the internal act, which Aquinas says is related to the external act as its form. This means that its moral nature is conferred on the external act by the internal act, which is to say by the end and intention of the agent. Prior to, or apart from, any consideration of the agent's intention *the external act is neither morally good nor morally evil because it lacks all moral character.*[10] For Aquinas, prior to factoring in the intention of the agent, the external act in question is amoral. This puts Aquinas closer to Abelard, as we have noted, and in the camp of those who deny that human acts can be intrinsically good or evil from the moral point of view. That this is the real teaching of Aquinas is the primary discovery of the revisionists, who make their case with great persuasiveness, relying heavily on the texts of Aquinas himself.[11]

But there is more. In addition to talking about the relationship between the internal and external acts as that of matter and form, Aquinas also speaks of them as being related as end and means. The external act is the means whereby the end or intention of the will is accomplished. And again, despite the fact that he is well aware of what the tradition holds, he maintains that the means takes its moral character from the end.[12] So it would be inconsistent, from Aquinas' point of view, to attempt to determine the morality of the means taken in itself.

The exterior act, then, whether it is viewed as the matter which the interior act of the will informs, or whether it is seen as the means used to achieve the end of the interior act of the will, is without moral character or interest *until that which gives it its moral character is factored into the equation,* and that is of course, the end or intention of the agent. Both lines of reasoning arrive at the very same conclusion, namely that human acts only become part of the moral universe due to the goodness or malice of the agent's intention. It is therefore inappropriate to speak of external acts as having an intrinsic moral character, be it good or bad. That was the view of Aquinas when he spoke in his own name, and it remained his own personal view until the very end.

2. *Contemporary Significance of the Revisionist View*

What difference, you may ask, does this make when considering the contemporary moral issues raised by the biological revolution and all the attending new technologies? The revisionist perspective gives one a sense that there may be a Catholic moral position which is not as absolutist as the traditional position appears to be. That it is possible to enter into "dialogue" with non-believers over these issues, without having to simply invoke the "intrinsically evil act argument" at the outset. It also allows us to search for ways to respond to the Marxian and Sartrean criticisms of our age, that as Catholics we are obliged to underestimate human dignity and responsibility. For as the current commitment within the Catholic church to peace and justice issues clearly demonstrates, believers can be as committed to transforming the world as they are to saving their souls.

Indeed, the Gospel message of "the Kingdom" makes taking responsibility for changing the world for the better a "precondition" for that salvation. And finally, the revisionist Catholic approach to morality has a better "fit" with regard to many contemporary experiences, all the while keeping faith with the true spirit, if not the letter, of the Catholic tradition. What recommends it to many Catholics is that it is less counter-intuitive at key junctures than is the tradition. How and why that is the case, can perhaps best be seen for considering two particular issues which clearly mark the difference between the revisionist and the traditional views. The distinction between "ontic" and "moral" evil; and the meaning and implementation of the principle of the double effect.

a. *Ontic Evil vs. Moral Evil*

Evil is one of those things which everyone can easily recognize in the concrete but which is rather difficult to describe or define in the abstract. Still the effort must be made. For our purposes here, it is sufficient to divide evil into two sorts. The first could be called "ontic" evil, or "physical" evil, or "pre-moral" evil, to designate that it is different from "moral" evil. What are the ontic or pre-moral evils of life?[13] Why everyone agrees: all those things which violate and frustrate vital human needs, desires and interests. This is not very helpful, however, because it remains too abstract and general. More specifically, the ontic, pre-moral evils of life are: DEATH, PAIN, DISABLEMENT, DEPRIVATION OF PLEASURE, DEPRIVATION OF FREEDOM & OPPORTUNITY, and DEPRIVATION OF ONE'S SELF-WORTH, DIGNITY OR SELF-ESTEEM.[14]

If you ask me how I know that these things "are evil," my only response is that they just are, and that everyone is well aware of that fact and that it requires no proof. Indeed, all six of those things are so objectively evil (that is to say evil in themselves, not evil merely from this person's or that person's point of view) that anyone who sought those things because she thought them desirable would be locked up as crazy. All six of those things ARE evil, that's just the way it is. So true is that, that a good rule of thumb would be that those six items represent the major evils of human life and all the other things we humans consider to be evil are thought to be so only because they introduce one or more these six basic evils into our lives.

All other things being equal, no one in her right mind would desire any one of the items on our list. But sometimes all other things are not equal. Take death for example. It is first on the list because it is the evil most destructive of vital human needs, desires and interests. Leaving faith out of it, death puts an end to all human projects or goals, it eradicates all interests, it quiets all desires, and it ends all relationships. It is therefore the supreme natural evil because it deprives us of every other good. But it is only the supreme natural evil—*all other things being equal.* A person can be in such unrelenting pain that death may be sought as a release from some other item on our list. That fact, however, does not make death a good to be sought in ordinary circumstances.

Similarly, we may submit to pain, disablement and a temporary deprivation of our freedom in the form of cancer surgery, or limb amputation, in order to avoid death. Here again, we seek some of the items on our list of evils in order to avoid others on that list. This does not mean that the items we now seek have somehow suddenly become goods. Not at all. They remain ''ontic evils.'' That's what makes human life oftentimes so tragic. We are forced to embrace one or more evils on our list in order to escape greater evils on our list. Were the items on our list not actually, really and objectively evil, even when we are forced by circumstances to choose them, there would be no ambiguity, no tragedy for us humans in the choosing of them. But tragedy there is, and in abundance.

This means that evil is only possible because we humans are the sorts of beings we are. We can die, and we don't want to. We can experience pain, and we don't want to. We can experience disablement, and we don't want to. We can be deprived of pleasure, and we don't want to be. We can be deprived of freedom, and we don't want to be. We can be deprived of our self-esteem, and we surely don't want to be. Those things, and all the others that lead to them, are called ''evils'' because they *deprive human beings of what they need for their lives and for their growth and development as persons.* For convenience, we call all such things ONTIC or PRE-MORAL EVILS.

Of course we can suffer "ontic evils" in many different ways. We can be deprived of our vital needs by floods, tornadoes, epidemics and other natural disasters, as well as by misfortunes such as industrial accidents and plane crashes. So the presence of "ontic evils" does not always indicate the presence of moral evil.

But when such deprivation of persons is brought about by the free and conscious decision and action of human beings, and in such a way as to be unjustified, *then, and only then, are we face to face with MORAL EVIL.* What that comes down to is this: Moral evil always involves an unjustified infliction by one person of one or more of the ontic evils on another. This leads to the obvious principle: NO UNJUST INFLICTION OF ONTIC EVIL—THEN NO MORAL EVIL EITHER. Moral evil, then, is simply the name we give to our voluntary, deliberate and unjustified increase of ontic evil in our world.

I would assume that thus far, both the traditionalists and the revisionists would generally agree. But when it comes to explaining what it is that makes the infliction of ontic evil "unjustified," they begin to part company. For example, intentionally taking an innocent life is, according to the tradition, always morally wrong, period. One cannot even begin to ask what would justify such an act, because as we have seen it is intrinsically evil, and therefore is beyond any sort of justification. So says the tradition.[15]

As would be expected from what we have already seen, the revisionists take a slightly different approach. If one describes an act performed by someone as "taking an innocent human life,'' without any reference to the agent's will or intention, one has yet to enter the world of morality. If one insists on calling an act so described ''evil,'' one must be speaking of an ''ontic'' or ''pre-moral'' evil, and there is no disagreement at all over the fact that killing someone is evil in that sense. Whether it is also ''morally'' evil depends on factors other than the objective description of the act. Those factors are, as I am sure the reader is by now tired of hearing, the subjective and intentional state of the agent's will. Until those are factored in one has yet to enter the realm where moral evil can even exist.

If we grant the revisionists their point that taking an innocent human life is pre-moral, how would they go about determining whether in a concrete case it was moral or immoral? By inspecting two aspects of the act to determine whether there was, according to reason, *a true proportion* between the interior act of will and the exterior act of taking an innocent human life. It is this concern for a proper proportion in accord with reason, which accounts for the fact that the revisionists are more frequently referred to as proportionalists.

Spinning off of Aquinas' notion that the internal will act is the form which gives the externally executed act its moral nature, the revisionists are anxious to know whether that external act offers apt matter (in Aquinas' terminology *materia apta*). Of course, if the will of the agent ''intends'' evil, then no matter is *apta*, and the act is immoral from the start. But if the intention is good, the act may still be immoral if there is not a proper proportion between the good intention and the external act. Clearly, the revisionist account opens the way for us to get beyond the ''intrinsically evil'' tag for an external act, and allows us to continue the dialogue factoring in the intention of the agent, and raising questions about apt matter. Its answers, therefore, may not be as definitive and clear as those of the tradition, but for many they seem to be more human.

The second proportion which must be checked out to see whether an act is immoral or not, stems from the alternate way Aquinas has of viewing the relationship between the internal and external acts, namely as end and means. And in that context, one must discern whether the external act is really an appropriate means, again according to reason, for accomplishing the intended end. If there is a contradiction involved, due to the fact that the means chosen may at first appear to be appropriate, but looked at in a wider more total perspective are seen to really violate and contradict the end, then the act will be judged immoral. And it will be so judged because it only apparently achieves the end.

For the revisionists, then, to justify an action is to assess these two proportionalities within the human act as being appropriate, in accord with right order and reason. From their perspective, it is sometimes justified to inflict "ontic" evil, and so there can be no absolute prohibition against doing so. This is especially clear when we come to discuss the principle of the double effect.

b. *The Principle of the Double Effect*

Life is never simple, and sometimes the actions we perform have more than the good effect we intend; they inflict ontic evil in some measure as well. The tradition has always been sensitive to this ambiguity of the human condition, and its account of the "principle of double effect" was meant to assuage undue anxiety among people over that fact. If the fact that we cause some evil when we act were definitive, we could scarcely act at all. The principle of "double effect" or of the "indirect voluntary" allows life to go on without moral scruple. But it is a complicated principle which can only be effectively invoked if it is properly understood.

The traditional understanding of the double effect principle is based on the fact that evil may never be directly willed. For to intend evil is to vitiate the whole act making whatever else is good about it irrelevant. So the double effect principle can only apply when an act has two effects of which one is the intended good effect, and the evil effect is unintended, and an incidental by-product of the act. When those general conditions are met, the double effect principles says that such an act may be performed morally if all of the following four specific conditions are also met.

1) The act to be done must be good in itself or at least indifferent.

2) The good intended must not be obtained by means of the evil effect.

3) The evil effect must not be intended for itself but only permitted.

4) There must be a proportionately grave reason for permitting the evil effect.

The first condition cannot be met on revisionist terms, because as we have seen acts in and of themselves have no moral dimension, deriving their moral character from relation to the agent's intention. But in traditional terms we can understand what it means, the act (object) used to produce the two effects must be either intrinsically good or at least indifferent.

The second condition requires that the two effects not be related to one another as cause and effect, that is each must be an effect of the same act, and the good effect cannot come about *by means of* the evil effect. Were that to be the case, then the good effect would be achieved by an evil means, the evil effect, and a good end never justifies an evil means. The good achieved by the act can never come about through the evil inflicted.

Thirdly, the agent may not intend the evil effect, but must intend only the good one. For to intend evil always introduces malice into the act, vitiating it from the start. The evil effect must be permitted or tolerated, never directly chosen.

The final condition to be met requires that there be a proportionately grave reason for allowing or permitting the evil effect. It is immoral to perform an act the good effect of which is slight, and the evil effect of which is very great. There is no due proportion *between the two effects,* that is they are not nearly equivalent. If the good were slight and the evil great, one could hardly call the evil effect "incidental."

That is the traditional account of the double effect principle. One can see, according to the conditions laid down, why the church cannot condone even saving the life of an expectant mother by aborting the unborn. While some may accuse the church of sexism in that case, the fact is that the traditional Catholic position has always rested on this double effect principle. Clearly, the good effect of saving the mother is produced through the bad effect of killing the unborn. And even though there is a proportion of a life against a life, the act is prohibited because the other conditions of the double effect principle are not fulfilled. And for an act to be moral according to the principle of double effect, *all* the above conditions must be met, as the tradition holds they clearly are in the case of a surgeon amputating a cancerous leg in order to save the life of the patient.

Aquinas[16] and the revisionists[17] see the double effect principle in a different way. Aquinas writes:

> Of course nothing prevents a single act from having a twofold effect, only one of which is in intention (*in intentione*), the other of which is beyond intention (*praeter intentionem*). Now moral acts take their species (i.e. their morality) from that which is truly intended, not obviously from that which is beyond intention since that is merely accidental. A double effect can follow from the act of one defending herself: one the conservation of one's own proper life, the other the killing of the assailant. Now an act of this sort does not become immoral (illicit) from the fact that one intends to preserve her own life, since it is natural to a living thing that it as much as possible conserve itself in existence. However, it is still possible that an act issuing from a good intention be rendered immoral (illicit) if it is not proportioned to the end. And therefore if someone uses more force than is necessary in defending her own life, the act would be immoral (illicit). If, however, the use of force is moderate, then it would be an act of licit self-defense.

The words are pretty much the same, but a careful reading shows that Aquinas is not presenting the traditional view here, but is rather re-affirming his own position that the morality of an act depends primarily on the intention of the agent. Even in the case of a twofold effect, one good the other not, one must factor in the agent in order to determine the moral character of the act.

The first condition put forth by the tradition, that an act be good or indifferent in itself and not evil, cannot apply in Aquinas' understanding of the matter, because acts in and of themselves have no moral character. Nor is Aquinas concerned with the second condition, as to whether the evil effect is a means to the good effect, since as we have already seen the morality of the means is determined by the intention of the agent and by whether that intention is in accord with right reason. The third condition is irrelevant, because the means is never intended for its own sake, and is, precisely as means, always intended only in relation to the end. The fourth condition speaks of a proper proportion between the two effects, and while Aquinas agrees it is necessary to speak of a proportion, it is not the one that exists between the two effects, but rather the one that must exist between all the elements of the act and the end or intention, and between the end or intention and right reason.

While the traditional account may speak of justifying mutilating someone in order to save her life on the principle of the double effect, Aquinas would say that there is no need to justify an act of mutilation precisely because in this case *there is no mutilation.* The good intention of the agent so permeates the act that from the moral point of view there is only one act, it is entirely good, and there is no moral evil involved at all.

By holding that acts have an intrinsic moral character, the tradition makes it easy for itself in judging the difficult cases which life inevitably presents. Aquinas and the revisionists say that it is not that simple. Acts are not in themselves moral or immoral, their morality depends on the intention of the agent, and whether that intention is conformed to right reason. This alternate approach, while presently under suspicion, gives us Catholics the opportunity to engage in meaningful dialogue with non-believers on the moral issues surrounding the new biology.

Of course, it does not follow that the revisionist view will always lead to conclusions which are contrary to the tradition. The reverse is more often the case. But at key junctures in the present dialogue over revolutionary bio-medical procedures, revisionism can bring to bear not only the wisdom of the tradition, but the wisdom of our present experience as well. It is to some of those thorny issues that we now turn.

NOTES TO CHAPTER III

1. Contemporary philosophy is generally divided up into Anglo-American and European or Continental philosophy. In ethics, the Anglo-American school is generally pragmatic and utilitarian, while the Continental school tends to be more phenomenological in its approach. Both schools present a challenge to the traditional Catholic moral position, but here we are chiefly considering the challenge which arises from a phenomenological approach to the human person and her mysterious freedom.

2. For this section I have been strongly influenced by a marvelous talk given in Milwaukee by Donald Monan, S.J., to the Vocations Directors of America back in 1966. It was entitled: *Freedom's Role In Constituting Vocations.* At the time he was Chairperson of the Philosophy Department at Le Moyne College.

3. I prefer to call these theologians "revisionist" primarily because they are revising our understanding and interpretation of the greatest moral thinker in the Catholic tradition, i.e. Thomas Aquinas. If the revised view is correct, that would mean that when the tradition invokes Aquinas to substantiate the position that certain human acts are intrinsically *(per*

se) evil, it errs. That strikes me as most significant. When these thinkers are called "proportionalists," as they are by Rome, it is meant to signify a foundational aspect of their thought, namely that before one can determine the morality of an act, one has to see if there is a proper proportion between the end of the act, and the means employed to achieve it. In any event, Charles Curran could well be said to be a proportionalist, which is why he is currently in such disfavor with Rome. Other "revisionist" moral theologians are: Richard McCormick, S.J., Louis Janssens, Peter Knauer, S.J., Bruno Schuller, S.J., and Joseph Fuchs, S.J. A good introduction to the problem can be gotten from the readings in: *Readings In Moral Theology No. 1,* edited by Charles Curran and Richard McCormick, S.J., Paulist Press, New York, 1979.

4. Cf. Dom Odon Lottin, *Morale Fondamentale,* Desclee, Paris, 1954, pp. 268-270, and pp. 279-281.

5. "So the personal thought of Aquinas cannot be doubted. Thomas found himself facing a scholarly tradition which ranked, with various reservations, the end of the agent (*finis operantis*) among the "circumstances" of the human act. Supremely respectful of "authorities" Thomas did not want to directly contradict them. STILL IT MUST BE NOTED THAT HE ONLY HOLDS TO THEIR LANGUAGE STRICTLY WHEN HE TREATS THE CIRCUMSTANCES OF THE HUMAN ACT. *In all other contexts,* he magnifies the influence of the end of the agent (*finis operantis*): the "intention" defines the human act, not only the internal act but also the external act, since it is nothing other than the object of the internal act. It is clear from a simple reading of his texts that *this* was his own personal position on the matter." Lottin, *op.cit.*, p. 270.

6. You will find Aquinas coping with the Catholic moral tradition and yet cautiously making his own very personal contribution along the way in the initially somewhat confusing yet ultimately clear readings to be found in *Summa Theologiae* I-II, Q. 18-20. Cf. also Daniel Maguire, *Moral Choice,* Doubleday, New York, 1978, p. 124, note #11, and p. 118.

7. My Aquinas teacher, Ignatius Eschmann, O.P., not only quoted this text, he made it the centerpiece for a presentation he made back in 1957 to the American Catholic Philosophical Association. Commenting on our text on that occasion he wrote:

   "With this statement, St. Thomas took his first step into the field of moral doctrine. Did he watch his step? We may be sure that he did. But might it not be profitable for us to watch him being careful about his first step? There seems to be something surprising, not to say disquieting, about this introduction to the second part of the *Summa*. It clearly implies the affirmation of man's autonomy. Evidently, St. Thomas is not concerned to present this autonomy as a mere relative privilege, valid only in subordination to God. In fact, he does *not* say: Man is the principle of his actions 'under God.' Rather he says: 'Man is the principle of his actions like God, like God's image.' On the basis of this initial statement, St. Thomas' moral doctrine has rightly been qualified as the doctrine of man's grandeur and independence, and has been contrasted with other types of moral thinking which insist on man's dependence and smallness."

   "St. Thomas' Approach To Moral Philosophy," *Proceedings of the American Catholic Philosophical* Association, Vol. XXXI, (1957), pp. 25-26.

8. *Summa Theologiae,* I-II, 19, 1, c.

9. *Ibid.*, 19, 1, ad 1 & ad 3; and 19, 3, c; and 19, 3, ad 1.

10. *Summa Theologiae,* I-II, 1, 3, ad 2; 1, 4; 8, 2; 17, 4; 20, 1-6.

11. Cf. Louis Janssens, "Ontic Evil and Moral Evil" in Curran & McCormick, *Readings In Moral Theology No. 1,* Paulist Press, New York, 1979, pp. 40-93. And in that same volume, Joseph Fuchs, S.J., "The Absoluteness of Moral Terms," pp. 94-137.

12. *Summa Theologiae* I-II, 6, 2; 8, 2; 18, 4, c, and ad 2.

13. I have treated this matter elsewhere in greater detail, cf. *Morality And Its Beyond,* Twenty-Third Publications, Mystic, 1984, pp. 30-34.

14. Looking at this list of ''ontic'' or ''pre-moral'' evils, one can easily see why it is not appropriate to call them ''physical'' evils though most of them are. The fact is, not all of them are, e.g. loss of self-worth, or self-esteem. Thus ''ontic'' or ''pre-moral'' are to be preferred as the designations of these real evils in life.

15. I have elsewhere addressed that traditional view, cf. May, William & Westley, Richard, *The Right To Die,* Thomas More, Chicago, 1980. Also *Morality And Its Beyond,* Twenty-Third Publications, Mystic, 1984, pp. 233-246.

16. *Summa Theologiae* II-II, 64, 7, c.

17. Peter Knauer, S.J., ''The Hermeneutic Function of the Principle of Double Effect,'' pp. 1-39, in Curran & McCormick, *Readings In Moral Theology No. 1,* Paulist Press, New York, 1979.

Appendix To Chapter Three
Aquinas On The Role of the Body in Human Life

THOMAS AQUINAS is, obviously, a very fine philosopher and theologian. But even such great thinkers as Aquinas are not equally talented and insightful in all areas of thought. In Aquinas' case, there are three areas in which his work bears the marks of genius. The first is the abstract and rarefied atmosphere of his metaphysics; the other two are more concrete and more subject to experiential verification, but they are areas in which his thought reaches the heights of genius. His moral theory is second to none, and in my judgment transcends the other two ethical giants, Aristotle and Kant, by quite a bit. But it is his genius with respect to the metaphysics of the human person that I want to bring to the reader's attention in this appendix. For if we are going to talk about the morality of technologies which impact particularly on human life, it would be well for us to have some sense of what that life is. On that issue, none of the traditionally great thinkers has done as well as Aquinas, his genius there can be life-giving. Had the Catholic tradition only taken his views on this matter more to heart, we might not have been plagued by Jansenism, and other spiritualisms which have made it difficult for Catholics to be fully human without feeling guilt. But alas, as was true regarding the intrinsic morality of acts, the Catholic tradition, to its detriment, opted to go another route.

What It Means To Be "Incarnate Spirit"

In order to get some feel for Aquinas' genius on the "human," we shall have to spend some time reflecting on the human condition, entering, as briefly and painlessly as I can manage it, the obfuscating world of his metaphysics. But bear with me, because the insight is crucial and fascinating, and it changes how one thinks of the human person. But if you think that because the insight originated with Thomas Aquinas that makes it a traditional view, you would be quite wrong. The truth is that Aquinas' genius has been ignored on this issue, and I am confident that were that not the case we would have a somewhat different view of what is and is not proper in the field of medical technology.

For Aquinas, human beings are not animals, not even "rational" ones. Though he accepted the Aristotelian definition of the human person, he did not think that "animal" was our proper genus metaphysically speaking. No. If one wants to classify humans metaphysically, one has no alternative but to eschew the genus "animal" for the more appropriate genus "spirit." The specifying difference distinguishing human beings from "pure" spirits is that we are "incarnate," that is to say "enfleshed" spirits. To place human beings in the genus "animal" is to commit a category mistake. It is to be fooled by appearances, by the fact that, like the higher animals we have a genotype, visceral organs, genitals and a digestive tract. But the significance of that similarity is misplaced and lost, unless one has some notion of the overall economy of the human person, an economy which Aquinas consistently taught was *totally spiritual.*

According to the Platonic account, which became the Christian account since all of the Church Fathers were Platonists, matter lies completely outside the domain of spirit. Even when they are joined, it is only by accident, that is because of a fall of some sort on the part of spirit. And so the war between them goes on. The human soul/spirit is hampered and at risk while in matter, and so death is the liberation of the human spirit from the prison of the body. Aquinas sees it otherwise.

For him, human beings are all and totally spirit, but are lowest in the order of spirits. That is to say, human beings are so low in the order of spirits that *in order to perfect themselves as spirit, they must be immersed in matter. Far from being a hindrance to spirit, matter is humankind's means of reaching spiritual perfection.* Soul and body are joined in so intimate a union within the human person, that Aquinas says not only does the human soul make the body live, it makes the body live by the soul's own spiritual life. Despite all appearances to the contrary there is none other than a spiritual life in human beings. And in that one life, the role of the human body is precisely to enable the human spirit to do the work of spirit. Aquinas really means what he says. So true is it that matter/body is essential to the spiritual perfection of an "incarnate spirit,'' that death is not in itself a liberation of the human spirit, but is its impoverishment. Without body, the human spirit cannot operate as spirit at all, cannot do the work of spirit, and so Aquinas felt that God would by Divine Influx make up to the impoverished human spirit for the lack of its body—at least until they were once again rejoined at the end.

Aquinas' position is so radical and revolutionary that to this day it has not gained anything like widespread acceptance. Yet if it is true, and I believe it is, it changes the Christian perspective on the human.

Aquinas identifies the ''work of spirit'' as knowing/understanding and loving. On his hypothesis, it follows that human beings can do neither without body. All attempts by humankind at a purely spiritual knowing or loving are not only wrong-headed, but futile. If we aspire to know and love each other, if we aspire to really be present to one another, then we must understand that as ''incarnate'' spirits we can only do that physically, incarnately, enfleshedly. More than that, if we aspire to know and love God, even then we can only do so incarnately, through our bodies. That is the price we pay for being lowest in the order of spirits. But fear not, the human body was created and fashioned as it is, precisely to enable and empower us to be fully human and to do the work of reconciliation, the very work of spirit. The human body, as anyone who has worked in health care knows, is marvelously suited to its ''spiritual'' tasks. It is not only a ''biological'' wonder, it is a ''spiritual'' marvel as well.

Consider the human face. In the human face more than anywhere else we encounter the mystery of our humanness: PRESENCE. It is there that we encounter the wonder of spirit-enfleshed. It is in the countenances of one another; in the eyes, the smile, the look, the glance, that we either see the invitation to live out our relatedness and bondedness to one another, or the fearful rejection of that dream. And the human voice, which issues from that face is itself an instrument of spirit. A word, a phrase, a tone all communicate in hidden ways what lies beneath the surface in the very heart and soul and spirit of a human being. And what of the human hand as an instrument of spirit? The warm firm grasp of hands in friendship, the caressing hands of lovers, the caring hands of those who minister to human needs, the helpful hands of neighbors, the prayerful hands of worship. . . all convey a reality which goes far beyond the physical.

But there is a deadly trade-off built into the bargain. Aquinas asked why it was that an immortal soul should be joined to an organic body. Wouldn't it be better if an incarnate spirit were joined to matter which more closely resembled it in indestructibility? Why not an inorganic body of granite, of diamonds? His answer is that in order to give the lowest sort of spirit access to knowledge and love a body is needed that is equipped with sense organs, and even sex organs. The consequence of that, of course, is that it is fragile and has only the most precarious of holds on existence. So the paradox of a spirit having to face death, is itself the direct result of that spirit's need to be ''incarnate'' in order to be about the work of spirit. For human beings, then, death is not a merely biological phenomenon, it too is the work of spirit. Even the fact *that* we die is not solely for biological reasons, because for Aquinas even death is part of the spiritual economy of an incarnate spirit. *How* we die, and *how* we live, is the work of spirit, and any discussion of bio-medical technologies needs believers to participate in order to make that point.

Conclusion

Given what has been said, *we have only two things at our disposal with which to do the work of the spirit,* to do the work of presence, to do the work of relatedness, love and solidarity, to do the work of the Kingdom. And when Jesus was among us, though God he be for Christians, he too, as human and an incarnate spirit, had only those same two things with which to accomplish his mission of reconciliation among us. And what are these two things ? Why our *WORDS* and *PHYSICAL PRESENCE,* of course.

And to this day those are the only things we humans have both for mediating the superabundance of God's unconditional love for humankind to one another, and for hastening the coming Kingdom and thus taking responsibility for our world, as Marx and Sartre have urged us. We make an abiding mistake, and sorely deceive ourselves whenever we think otherwise.

We are NOT animals! We are not biological specimens! Aquinas gives us an illuminating account of why our bodies cannot be reduced to biological resources for those with money and power to exploit for their own purposes. We are spirits! Called to be responsible for our world, and called also to witness to the unique and precious dignity of each one. We may be appalled by the realities of the new bio-medical technology, and frightened by the even more startling accomplishments that are foretold. But we must transcend our revulsion and our fear, and speak words of hope and dignity in faith. These troubled times call for no less. And it is to that task that we now turn.

CHAPTER FOUR
Reproductive Technologies and Human Embryo Research

BIO-MEDICAL ethics has become in the past decade a truly international (worldwide) interest. Science and the biomedical technology it has spawned know no national boundaries, and so have spread throughout the world, especially in the advanced industrial nations. As evidence of the unity of humankind, wherever they have spread they have not only raised moral dilemmas, but have raised the same moral dilemmas. However diverse the cultures involved, it is uncanny to note how people in every country raise the same moral issues, and following the secular bent of Western culture these days, have by and large given the *same* reasoned answers. Just one more indication of how wrong-headed ethical relativism is even in a secular context.

The common and recurring issues regarding human reproduction which give rise to much discussed moral dilemmas are: In Vitro Fertilization (IVF), Artificial Insemination by Donor (AID), Embryo Transfer (ET), Surrogate Motherhood, and Human Embryo Experimentation and Research. National Commissions have been set up in all the industrial nations to present governments with appropriate recommendations and guidelines for public policy concerning these matters, and a review of them indicates a worldwide consensus.[1]

Leaving faith aside, and within a purely secular context, reasonable women and men are generally in favor of artificial insemination by donor, and *in vitro* fertilization, and are generally wary of or against surrogate motherhood, embryo transfer, and experimentation and research on human embryos. When we factor in Catholic faith, we find that the Catholic church is categorically against all five.[2] But it is interesting to note that when the church speaks out against three of the five issues mentioned, she speaks not only for herself, not even only for believers, but also for a majority of secular men and women as well. So in our day, as has been the case in every preceding age, the Catholic church continues to lead the way in behalf of all of humankind in championing respect for the sacredness of human life. It has ever been thus. As we have seen, *that's* the Catholic tradition.

Of course in a secular age such as ours, there are always those who reject a position simply because it arises from the context of faith. Such people reject any position put forth by the Catholic church. They assume out of hand that it must be antiquated. Still the call of the church for cooperation from non-believers in stemming the growing dehumanization of our day has the ring of truth to it:

> The rapid development of technological discoveries gives greater urgency to this need to respect the criteria just mentioned: science without conscience can only lead to man's ruin. "Our era needs such wisdom more than bygone ages if the discoveries made by man are to be further humanized. For the future of the world stands in peril unless wiser people are forthcoming" (*Gaudium Et Spes*, #15).[3]

Still, while thoughtful women and men dialogue and attempt to stop the growing dehumanization of our times, bio-science and its subsequent technologies seem blissfully to go on, unmindful of the dire consequences for humankind of what they do. They seem to have a life of their own. A life which seems to be on the verge of becoming beyond all human control.

1. *The Elan of Technology*

A classic example of this can be seen in the history of amniocentesis. Amniocentesis is the procedure originally developed to identify fetuses with severe genetic disorders so that they might be treated early, *in utero.* The procedure consists of drawing a sample of the amniotic fluid surrounding the fetus and analyzing it for the telltale signs of genetic disorder. The test is also able to determine the sex of the fetus as well. If the tests are positive for genetic disorders, then therapeutic measures can often be initiated to improve the prospects of the unborn child. All of the science and technology that have informed physicians of what to look for in the amniotic fluid, and the clinical procedures for drawing same, were all aimed at benefiting the patient, i.e. the unborn child. The inauguration of this procedure around 1975 was heralded as a great breakthrough and a substantial benefit to the unborn. And so it is.

At the beginning, since putting a syringe into the amniotic sack is not without risk to the unborn, however slight, something can always go wrong, the procedure was limited to pregnant women who had previously given birth to genetically defective children, or who were known to be at risk of doing so. After the procedure became more known and more widely used, it was made available as a matter of course to older pregnant women who were statistical risks because of their age. Thus far the procedure itself presents no moral difficulties, although sometimes the information gotten occasions not treatment of a defective fetus, but its abortion. Still the decision to undergo the procedure does not involve nor necessitate that one make the decision to abort. That is a separate issue. But as time has passed, pressure has increased for the medical profession to allow all pregnant women access to the procedure, so that they may know the gender of the child they carry. It is now claimed that all pregnant women, married or single, "have a right" to amniocentesis and the information it can give.

So we see how medical procedures have a dynamism or elan of their own, and what starts out as a procedure for one purpose in actual practice comes to be seen by others as something which can help them achieve their own purposes as well. Scientific knowledge and the medical procedures it generates are in the public domain, and once there people claim the "right" to use both in order to achieve their own ends, ends not intended, even if foreseen, by those who tested and perfected the procedures in the first place.

Of course, the new technologies are frightfully expensive, and insurance companies are reluctant to cover people for what they viewed at first as "experimental" procedures, and later when no longer experimental, as at least unusual and uncommon. So, though the argument is made that all have a "right" to these new technologies, in actual fact only those in the best of economic situations can afford them. Pressure is then put on governments to make these wondrous new technologies available to all its citizens. That then raises the issue of whether public support ought to be given to such procedures, especially when they are viewed by many as beyond the bounds of right reason and morality. The issues get very volatile indeed with respect to the new reproductive technologies, because, as we shall see, always lurking in the background is the ominous problem of abortion, about which this nation, and the world for that matter, remains painfully divided.[4]

2. *Artificial Insemination*

At first sight, there doesn't seem to be anything unreasonable or immoral about a couple wanting to have a child by artificial means when the natural method of sexual intercourse has proven ineffective. Indeed, for centuries there was only one way to conceive a child, and those who were unsuccessful at it were simply out of luck. One of the marvels of modern science is its ability to help nature along a bit, thus opening the possibility for natural parenthood to couples unable to conceive in the usual way.

Now, while in vitro fertilization is relatively recent, artificial insemination has been around for centuries (the first attempt at human artificial insemination dates from about 1799), and has been widely used with livestock and in animal husbandry generally. Artificial insemination (AI) consists of the mechanical (i.e. non-sexual) introduction of semen into the vagina or uterus in order to induce pregnancy. It has been widely used as a method to fight infertility in humans since about 1950. If the semen is from the husband, then we have *Artificial Insemination by Husband* (AIH). If from a sperm bank or from a third party donor, we have *Artificial Insemination by Donor* (AID).

People do not generally feel uncomfortable about medical science helping a couple circumvent their infertility problem if the semen of the woman's husband is used. But then why the need for a third party donor? Obviously, because the sperm of the husband is unsuitable for any one of a number of reasons. The husband may be infertile. Or he may have a known hereditary or genetic disorder which would adversely affect any child conceived from his sperm. Also, there may be a genetic mutation in the husband's sperm cells due to exposure to radiation, chemotherapy or other noxious agents. The couple wants a child of their own, and settle for having one who at least carries the genetic contributions of its mother. While generally accepting of AID, people are not as comfortable with it as with AIH, because it raises difficult questions about adultery, fidelity in marriage, and the effect on the child of discovering its origins.

3. *In Vitro Fertilization (IVF)*

However problematic artificial insemination may be, it is relatively simple in the sense that mother is still mother, and ambiguity only exists with respect to father. Who is father to this child? The genetic father (the semen donor) or the sociological father (the one who raises the child)? With the advent of the new reproductive technologies things become ever so much more complex, and we now have the know-how to produce a child with five parents. Count them. A genetic mother and a genetic father (those who contribute sperm and ova to the genetic make-up of the child); a gestational mother (the woman within whose womb the child was brought to term); and a sociological mother and a sociological father (those who ultimately raise the child). Given the present technology, it is not necessary that any one of the possible mothers or father be the same person. The new reproductive technologies are changing the very meaning of the words "mother" and "father" in our society. What confusion for the child!

If the technology of the 70's gave us sex without children, then the technology of the 80's makes it possible for us to have children without sex. Artificial fertilization, especially *in vitro* fertilization, allows for germline cells or gametes (sperm and ova) to be joined outside the body in the laboratory, and then when successful fertilization has occurred to transfer the zygote (fertilized cell formed from union of two gametes) to the woman's uterus for implantation (ET - embryo transfer) and hopefully a thereafter normal pregnancy. Since the so-called "genetic material" (gametes) can be gotten from any subjects and joined in the laboratory, and since the female donor need not necessarily be the one in whose womb the zygote is implanted, the possibilities are manifold. As of now, the gestational mother is still required, but scientists dream of the day when they will be able to join gametes in the laboratory and bring the child to term there as well in an artificial womb of some sort. The new reproductive technologies already give humans unprecedented control over the mechanics of reproduction, and promise to broaden it further in the coming decade. Joined with the newly emerging ability to alter the extracted genetic material *before* joining it, it would seem that soon we humans will have control of much more than the "mechanics" of reproduction.

Simply put, *in vitro* fertilization is the process whereby developing ova (plural) are first surgically removed from the ovary (laparoscopy). Each of the extracted eggs are joined with concentrated sperm sample in a culture dish and placed in an incubator for two and a half days. Several of the fertilized ova are drawn into a syringe and then inserted through the cervix into the uterus. If successful implantation occurs, the developing fetus is monitored for abnormalities and defects, and if brought to term is usually delivered by Cesarean section. To increase the possibility of successful implantation more than one zygote is introduced into the uterus, increasing the statistical possibilities of multiple births. As for the fertilized eggs remaining in the the laboratory dishes, they are usually frozen for future use in case the first attempt is unsuccessful.

As was the case with artificial insemination, *in vitro* fertilization can be either by spouses (AIH or perhaps better AIS) or by donor (AID). And as was the case with amniocentesis, once the technology for the IVF procedure is in place, people claim the "right" to use it for their own purposes. So it is that unmarried women who desire children but have no wish to be married and have a husband see IVF as their means of achieving that goal. So a procedure which was expressly developed to overcome sterility problems in married people, is now claimed as a right by those who, though not sterile, want children but do not want the personal involvements of marriage. The IVF technology makes it possible for them to have children in a sexless, non-relational way.

a. *The Morality of In Vitro Fertilization*

Obviously, the new reproductive technologies already in place, and those which are foreseen for the near future, are capable of transforming the traditional family structure. Do we really want to do that? Do we really want to change the traditional family by introducing a third genetic participant in reproduction? What will that do to the couple's relationship? What weight ought we to put on the intense desire for a child with the genes of at least one parent over against the psychological, and sociological ramifications of introducing a third party gamete into the family structure? What affect does all this have on the child? Are the parents' desires absolute, overriding all concerns for the effect of their actions on their offspring? These are just some of the weighty questions which reasonable people raise when assessing the morality of IVF. Answers are not so easy to come by, and consensual answers are almost impossible of achievement in a pluralistic and secular culture such as ours.

The cancer of "individualism" has so overtaken our age and society that moral issues, if they are even raised, are generally couched in the limiting terms of a person's individual rights. Since sterile couples have a right to children, it would be immoral to interfere with their attempts to take advantage of the new reproductive technologies. That is just about where the average American is on the issue. But even a cursory look at the situation as described above gives thoughtful and more morally sensitive people reason to pause. There is something about about IVF which just doesn't seem right, which just doesn't "fit."

If the procedure extracted one ovum, and if only one ovum was fertilized, and that fertilization achieved using the spouses sperm, common human reason[5] while not totally at peace would be generally affirming of the procedure. But, that is not the way it works. Many ova are fertilized, the "spare" ones are either immediately destroyed, used for scientific research, or frozen for future implantation or experimentation and ultimate destruction. Recognizing that fact, common human reason begins to sense the presence of disorder and the question of possible immorality is raised even in the secular context.

It should be noted that transferring the zygote from the laboratory disk to the uterus is not without risk. There is a great danger of genetic damage. This is seen as part of the trade-off in overcoming sterility, and should the zygote be damaged that fact can be determined by monitoring the developing fetus and aborting it if things should go wrong. In abortion-minded cultures like ours, that does not even raise a moral issue. After all, if the couple has a "right" to a child, it certainly has a "right" to a normal child, and should after all our machinations the child not be normal, we can always dispose of it and start over.

In addition to all those problems, there are the added problems raised by the use of donor sperm for the fertilization. The psychological and social ramifications of this procedure are not yet known, the number of so-called "test-tube" babies is as yet very small, but lack of hard knowledge about those effects creates a cultural atmosphere in which the procedure is allowed to go on. If it does unacceptable psychological harm to the marriage, to the child, we'll find that out in the future and then be able to react accordingly. For now, full steam ahead—in the name of science, in the name of technology, in the name of helping people overcome sterility. It is amidst and against this contemporary mind-set that the Catholic church attempts to bring to the situation an entirely different perspective and set of values.

b. *The Traditional Catholic Perspective*

Advances in reproductive technology have made it possible to procreate apart from the sexual relations of spouses, but what is technically possible may not be morally permissible. Reason must be brought to bear on the manifold issues which the new technology raises. We must be ever aware that we are concerned with the reproduction of "human" life, which is inviolable from the moment of conception until the moment of death. As "human" the transmission of this life is not a merely biological phenomenon. It is nature's (and God's) plan that human life be transmitted relationally, i.e. by the redemptive intimacy and sexual interaction in love of a man and woman joined together in a holy conjugal union. It is a violation of the natural order of things, therefore, to engage in reproductive technologies which violate these primary moral values surrounding the sacredness of human life. Each child has a universal human right to be conceived and brought into this world within the nurturing confines of a loving relation between spouses. Consequently, in vitro fertilization by donor (AID) violates the natural order of things and is always immoral.

Obviously, sterility can be particularly difficult for a loving couple which desires to have a child, but according to the Catholic tradition those laudable and subjectively good intentions cannot render AID in vitro fertilization conformable to right order and morality. It is objectively wrong, violating as it does the inalienable properties of marriage, as well as the rights of the offspring. The desire for a child is, of course, natural, and is often all the stronger if a couple is affected by sterility which appears permanent or incurable. Still, no one has a right to have a child, children are not property after all. Spouses have only the right to perform acts which lead to procreation. If that is not possible, then there are other ways, e.g. adoption, for the couple to fulfill their desire for children. Ways which do not violate the natural order of things.

Of course, it will immediately be asked whether IVF by spouse (AIS), where there is no third party donor, might not escape the Catholic objections to AID. If natural sexual intercourse is ineffective for a particular couple, is it not morally permissible for them to express their love for one another by giving life through IVF? After all, while it may be true that the child so conceived would not be directly the result of an act of sexual intercourse, throughout the marriage the spouses have expressed their love sexually, and will do so afterward as well. Isn't their love enough to transform the act of IVF into a procreative act worthy of human beings?

Expressly addressing that issue in 1987, the Congregation for the Doctrine of the Faith said:

> Conception *in vitro* is the result of the technical action which presides over fertilization. Such fertilization is neither in fact achieved nor positively willed as the expression and fruit of a specific act of the conjugal union. In homologous IVF (AIS), therefore, even if it is considered in the context of "de facto" existing sexual relations, the generation of the human person is objectively deprived of its proper perfection: namely that of being the result and fruit of a conjugal act. . . .[6]

It could hardly be clearer. Human reproduction, if it is to be moral in the traditional view, *must be the direct result of sexual intercourse between spouses.* All other methods of human reproduction are rejected on the grounds of violating the dignity of marriage, and the dignity and right of children to be conceived and born from a specific act of sexual love on the part of their parents. So even if all the other moral objections to IVF could be met, the procedure would still not be acceptable in traditional Catholic eyes because it circumvents sexual intercourse and is, therefore, against the natural order.

One need not be a believer to "feel" the overall power and wisdom of the traditional Catholic position on IVF. As we have seen, common human reason has raised many of the same difficulties with respect to IVF as the Catholic position has. But common human reason cannot accept the proposition that the *only* acceptable method of reproduction is through sexual intercourse. So the traditional Catholic view loses the support of most non-believers on that point. And while the revisionist position within the church for the most part agrees with the traditional position on IVF, it would want to make an "adjustment" with respect to this latter point.

c. *A Revisionist Adjustment*

On revisionist principles, we recall, no act is in and of itself immoral, since the act is not part of the moral universe unless and until one factors in the intention of the agent. Thus, to say that an act of human reproduction not the result of sexual intercourse is in itself immoral would not be agreed to by the revisionists. If at some future date reproductive technology advances to the point where spare fetuses do not result from IVF with all the moral complications that raises, on revisionist principles it would be acceptable in at least one case. That being the case of AIS.

The traditional position has expressly stated that no intention on the part of a couple, however good and noble, can make IVF morally acceptable because fertilization by mechanical means is *ipso facto* immoral. But simply saying that, does not make it so. The Catholic church may well wish it were that way, but as we saw in Chapter Three a strong case has been made by the revisionists that it is otherwise. And the sense that it is otherwise keeps secular common reason from agreeing as well.

New technologies put new possibilities within the reach of humankind. We human beings must assess what, if any, morally responsible use can be made of them. In making that judgment, we cannot simply say that because the new way is not the old way it is unacceptable. We must discern and evaluate the proper proportion between the agent's intention and right reason, and between the external act as the means of achieving the agent's intention and that intention.

With regard to human reproduction, sexual intercourse was for millennia the only means available, but that does not mean it is the only possible appropriate means to that end. And as the revisionists remind us, the morality of the now available alternate means must be carefully discerned and not simply rejected out of hand. That is too easy. If at some future date the unacceptable side effects now accompanying IVF, e.g. spare fetuses, etc., were bypassed, on revisionist principles IVF by spouse would be not only not immoral but a good and noble act. The generous and loving intention of the spouses would make it so. That conclusion better conforms to common human reason as well. Clearly a child has a right to be conceived in marriage and in love, but we seem to be stretching things a bit far when we say that a child also has the right to be conceived by an act of sexual intercourse.

So, it seems, that whether one is operating out of common human reason, the traditional Catholic position, or the revisionist position, one can raise substantive objections to the present medical practice of IVF, especially AID and the "sperm-bank" mentality. Clearly, on this issue we are face to face with limits. Unfortunately, the wisdom of the moral perspectives we have mentioned seems to be going unheeded as medical science and technology come more and more under the dominance and control of business. That may frighten and sadden us, but the apparent ineffectiveness of the call to proper limits does not relieve us of the obligation to speak our words of moral wisdom anyway. We must be sure to do that for our culture, trusting that in the end life and experience will reveal to all what faith and reason have revealed to us.

4. *Surrogate Motherhood*

Such revelations usually take some time, but the issue of surrogate motherhood is one which has totally turned around in five years. Acceptance for the practice is fast declining on all fronts, and states have begun to pass laws outlawing surrogacy contracts or declaring them invalid. Surrogacy was never a good idea, but it still has taken time for the nation to realize it. The case of Baby M (the Sterns vs. the Whiteheads) brought the matter to national attention, and the disorder of the whole surrogacy enterprise became immediately visible to all. In the wake of that national publicity, surrogacy in the United States is no longer a growing practice and can be expected to decline.

Surrogacy is just a special kind of artificial insemination, but done under contract for money, thus making it a legal nightmare as well. In cases where the woman is unable to be a gestational mother, her husband becomes the donor of sperm to be artificially introduced into a woman hired for that purpose. She then carries the child to term, and shortly after birth delivers up the child, according to the terms of the contract, to its genetic father and his wife, who then becomes its legal and sociological mother. What relation the "surrogate" mother has to the child thereafter varies, but the relationship is usually spelled out in great detail in the original contract.

Since Western culture had already accepted the use of third party donors for reproduction, the problematic issues about surrogacy did not center on that issue at all. Rather, because surrogacy was controlled by a pre-gestational agreement or contract, it was the legal issues on which people focused. Before the law, which of the women was "mother" to this child? In case of conflict, whose rights would prevail. Was the contract legally binding? That is to say, while it certainly might be possible to contract for gestational services, could such a contract validly abrogate the maternal rights of the surrogate? How did surrogacy differ from "selling babies"? And since babies are neither property nor services, how could they be bartered away in an economic arrangement in a nation which had fought the Civil War precisely to end such practices? Of course, underneath all of these legal issues lies the fundamental issue of the dignity of human persons and the dignity of the human reproductive process as well.

All these legal issues came to a head in the Baby M case, when the surrogate mother, Mary Beth Whitehead, had a change of heart and did not want to give up her baby to William and Elizabeth Stern who had contracted for her gestational services. As the case went to the courts, feminist voices were raised against surrogacy as the exploitation of women, especially women without marketable skills, indigent or in need of funds. Under such conditions they might well succumb to the temptation to enter into a dehumanizing surrogacy contract. And as is clear from the court records in the Baby M case, the courts seem more disposed to rule in favor of those with money.[7]

a. *The Morality of Surrogacy*

In many ways, surrogacy is really not morally problematic. It constitutes a violation of human dignity in so many different ways that the surprise is that it has been publicly advocated at all. It is judged negatively by secular common reason, by Catholic, traditional and revisionist, principles as well. That convergence of condemnation may not deter those whose self-interest lies in surrogacy, but it makes it more and more difficult to publicly advocate surrogacy as a morally and socially acceptable solution to infertility in this culture. It takes very little sensitivity to discern its disordered nature, and to foresee the devastating social and psychological effects on the children so conceived. Human beings are *not for sale.*

Having consistently proclaimed the dignity of persons and of the reproductive process within marriage in the issues of artificial insemination and IVF, the Catholic church was well positioned to judge the morality of surrogacy on those same principles. It did not have to wait to untangle the intricate legal issues involved, because it had already addressed the heart of the matter in terms of human reproduction, and therefore had only to reaffirm its stand. Some will say that this is simply an unwillingness on the part of the Catholic church to address contemporary issues, but the convergence of contemporary moral and legal thinking against surrogacy blunts that objection and confirms the wisdom of the traditional Catholic position on the matter.

5. *Human Embryo Experimentation*

Unfortunately, the growing moral consensus, which confirms the Catholic position on surrogacy and makes judging its morality relatively easy, does not follow over into other moral issues raised by the new reproductive technologies. We have already seen that in relation to IVF, and that is the case also with human embryo experimentation. In the past, experimentation on human embryos was not a real possibility except in the most clandestine of ways. After all, no one wanted medical personnel experimenting with "their baby." But IVF has depersonalized the whole thing, so that once gametes are gotten for in-laboratory use, it is possible for experimenters to fertilize more ova than they reveal to the donors, and then to use the zygotes thus created for their own purposes. That sounds dishonest and deceptive, but it has happened. When one is motivated by a thirst for more and more knowledge, and when so much money and prestige are at stake, we humans have a way of rationalizing our behavior unbelievably. The new reproductive technologies have made that sort of thing more easily possible.

True, hospitals and governments can lay down guidelines and set up oversight committees for such research, but one cannot monitor every researcher, at every moment, in every laboratory across the country. And in the wee hours of the morning when no one is around, what is to prevent the fertilization of ova, and the creation of zygotes to further the noble cause of science?

Catholics are offended by such thoughts, but for medical personnel for whom a human life is sacred and beyond tampering only once the fetus becomes viable, such actions and experimentation raise no moral issues at all.

Again, a medical technology created explicitly to achieve one end, overcoming infertility, once in the public domain, comes to be seen as a means to other ends. Indeed, having collected the "genetic material" to make IVF possible for a couple, the medical people can quite easily think that their success in helping the infertile couple makes them deserving of a reward. The reward of using some of that "genetic material" for *their* purposes. As anyone familiar with contemporary medicine knows, that is how it currently works in our country, which is also one reason why so much stress is put on informed consent in health care circles these days. There is so much secrecy not only because reputations and money are at stake, but also because many of the research practices are less than ethical or legal.

But fetal experimentation occurs not only in the laboratory setting; thanks to IVF, it occurs in clinical settings as well. Abortion clinics have a wealth of "specimens" if they so desire. Disposal of aborted fetuses from such institutions is not monitored, and arrangements can always be made with researchers for some of them. Indeed, researchers can actually place orders for the kinds of specimens they want. Spare IVF and aborted fetuses do not have the loving concern of anyone to protect them from any profanations which those in control of the situation might wish to visit upon them. So they are thought to be fair game for medical research uses. Since viability is the touchstone in this culture of when a fetus is due full "human" respect, and since the fetuses we have been talking about are not yet viable, it is thought to be in the interests of medical science and research to use them for experimentation. Of course, such arrangements are not much publicized, but again anyone knowledgeable about how things work these days is aware of them.

Finally, there are cases where experimental non-therapeutic procedures have been done on fetuses in the womb, when their mothers went in for their regular obstetric examinations. Again, since the Hippocratic Oath, in which the patient's welfare was the primary value to which all others yielded, is no longer in effect, sometimes the good of the individual patient is set aside for the general advancement of scientific knowledge and the good of future generations. Sometimes, such procedures may be done without the knowledge or consent of the patient.

a. *The Morality of Fetal Experimentation*

The traditional Catholic opposition to fetal experimentation is as absolute as its opposition to contraception and abortion. It is absolutely forbidden regardless of circumstances. The act is in and of itself immoral. Consistency requires the church to take that position.

If the fetus is to be respected as "human" from the moment of its conception, then it follows that experimentation without informed consent cannot be justified however noble the motive. To say otherwise would be to reduce the dignity of the human individual to one of utility for other people's purposes. In its 1987 statement, the Congregation for the Doctrine of the Faith expressly said:

> Medical research must refrain from operations on live embryos, unless there is a moral certainty of not causing harm to the life or integrity of the unborn child and the mother, and on condition

> that the parents have given their free and informed consent to the procedure. No objective, even though noble in itself, such as a foreseeable advantage to science, to other human beings, or to society can in any way justify experimentation on living human embryos or fetuses, whether viable or not, either inside or outside the mother's womb. The practice of keeping alive human embryos in vivo or in vitro for experimental or commercial purposes is totally opposed to human dignity.[8]

The absolute dignity of the human fetus from the moment of conception also requires that even diagnostic procedures be done within proper limits. Prenatal diagnostic testing, when it is aimed at safeguarding and healing the individual and respects the integrity of the embryo and fetus, is allowed. But when such testing is done with the express intention of aborting the fetus depending on the results of the test, it no longer is a therapeutic procedure respecting life but becomes a possible "death sentence" depending on the diagnosis. According to the Congregation of the Faith Instruction such prenatal diagnoses, though widely practiced, are intrinsically immoral and absolutely forbidden.[9]

It should be noted here that the traditional position on the issue of prenatal diagnostics gets very close, indeed, to the revisionist position. What makes the diagnostic procedure moral or immoral is the intention with which it is initiated and carried out, and whether there is a proper proportion between means and end, and between the end and "right reason." But that is just what the revisionists, following Aquinas, hold is the case with regard to *every* moral issue, not just this one.

While very respectful of the traditional position, revisionist,

Richard A. McCormick wonders whether Catholic principles require an absolute prohibition against fetal research. He suggests that there may be a way to keep faith with the Catholic tradition of respect for human life and yet allow for responsible research on fetuses in limited ways.[10] He in no way wants to condone the kinds of clandestine activities we mentioned above, nor does he want to prostitute the individual for some greater good for the whole, which is purely utilitarian and is to be rejected. But he feels that for the good of future generations of fetuses yet unborn, it just might be possible to approve of some fetal research in the present, if we analyze what we mean by *proxy consent* in cases of therapeutic intervention on fetuses.

According to the accepted medical practice and the Catholic tradition, as well, even when an experimental procedure is therapeutic, i.e. done for the well-being of the fetus, it can only be done with the informed consent of the parents, acting as proxies for the unborn fetus. McCormick suggests that the reason such parental consent is morally acceptable is because life and health are goods which the fetus *ought* to choose for itself if it were able, and so we accept the proxy choice of the parents on that ground. Since the fetus would want what was best for itself regarding life and health, it is perfectly acceptable for those charged and responsible for the life of the fetus to make the choice in its name.

Now, McCormick asks, are there not situations in which experimentation is something which the fetus ought to want just as it does life and health, and if so, he wonders, why wouldn't proxy consent by parents in that situation be the only condition required for experimentation to be a moral act? Are there not things which we ought to do for others simply because we are members of the human race? If we can be of help to others, and without running any great risks for ourselves and our loved ones, ought we not to do it? Do we not have an obligation to do our share so that others may prosper? If the experiments in question are such that they are the sorts of things which we all ought to do for the sake of the common good, then McCormick thinks that it is proper for parental/proxy consent to be given. To turn away would be the height of selfishness and a denial of our basic humanity.

Looked at in that way, the case could be made that precisely because the Catholic tradition holds that the fetus is human from the very first moment of its conception, that as part of that humanity it can be assumed that a fetus would want to do what any human would want to do to help others, and that it is therefore a good and truly human thing to have the fetus, by proxy consent, participate in an experiment which would benefit others. Far from reducing the fetus to a thing used to benefit others, this would underscore the tradition's constant affirmation of the humanity of the fetus.

But that line of reasoning does not open the door to any and every experiment. There are rational, right order limits which must be observed in this case, as in all cases of medical research and experimentation. The major limit is that the experimentation can pose no real discernible risk, as far as prudent human judgment can discern, to the fetus experimented on. Secondly, the research and experimentation must be legitimate and there must be a clear cut need for it. When these conditions are met, fetal experimentation seems to confirm the humanity of the fetus and its relatedness to the rest of the human race, rather than to violate it. Thus, an absolute prohibition of fetal experimentation is not the only attitude open to believers.

6. *Conclusion*

In a culture as pragmatic and utilitarian as our own, where bio-medical research is so lucrative, it is not popular to speak of limits and of the restrictions which our common humanity places upon us. Even if popular acceptance for moral wisdom is not likely, it is incumbent on those of us who believe and remain committed to "right order" to speak out in favor of the rational limits which are breached daily. In that task, the Catholic church as an "expert in humanity," continues to play an important role. If, at times, her wisdom is just a bit more rigid than common reason requires, there can be no doubt of the overall right-headedness of her position. She has demonstrated that marvelously in relation to the new reproductive technologies and, as we shall see in our concluding chapter, she does so also in relation to the issues of organ transplants, genetic engineering, and euthanasia.

NOTES TO CHAPTER IV

1. Hastings Center Report, Special Supplement—*Biomedical Ethics: A Multinational View,* Vol. 17, No. 3, June, 1987, pp. 6-7.

2. The official Catholic view is summed up with sensitivity and power in the Congregation For The Doctrine Of The Faith February 22, 1987 document: *Instruction On Respect for Human Life in Its Origin and on the Dignity of Procreation: Replies to Certain Questions of the Day,* United States Catholic Conference, Publication #156-3, Washington, D.C., 1987.

I have thematically excerpted portions of this document and you will find them as an appendix to this chapter. See also the Congregation's December 29, 1975 document: *Declaration on Certain Problems of Sexual Ethics,* in Austin Flannery, O.P., *Vatican Council II: More Post Concilar Documents,* Costello Publishing, Northport, New York, 1982, pp. 486-499.

3. *Instruction on Respect For Human Life. . ., op. cit.,* p. 10.

4. Just as I predicted it would be fifteen years ago when I wrote *What A Modern Catholic Believes About the Right to Life,* (Thomas More, Chicago, 1973), things are still pretty much just as they were then. The major difference is that abortion has become institutionalized and a taken for granted procedure, and the abortion mind-set of our day makes the *in vitro* fertilization procedure appear morally unproblematic to many.

5. When I speak of "common human reason," I mean to leave all religious or faith considerations aside, and am speaking in a secular context. If "common human reason" senses disorder, that means that objective women and men of no religious commitment discern a deviation from "right order" and hence immorality.

6. *Instruction On Respect for Human Life. . . op. cit.,* p. 30.

7. George J. Annas, "Baby M: Babies (and Justice) for Sale," *Hastings Center Report,* Vol. 17, no. 3, June, 1987, pp. 13-15.

8. *Instruction on Respect for Human Life. . . op. cit.,* p. 16. This view is also held by non-Catholics, see especially Paul Ramsey, "Shall We Reproduce? The Medical Ethics of In Vitro Fertilization," *Journal of the American Medical Association,* Vol. 220, no. 10, June 5, 1972.

9. *Instruction on Respect for Human Life. . . op. cit.,* p. 14-15.

10. Richard A. McCormick, "Fetal Research, Morality, and Public Policy," *Hastings Center Report,* Vol. 5, June 1975.

APPENDIX TO CHAPTER IV

Excerpts From:
Instruction on Respect for Human Life
In Its Origin and on the Dignity of Procreation:
Replies to Certain Questions of the Day,
Congregation for The Doctrine of the Faith 1987 document:
United States Catholic Conference
Publication #156-3, Washington, D.C., 1987

1. HUMANKIND'S RESPONSIBILITY FOR LIFE

The gift of life which God the Creator and Father has entrusted to man calls him to appreciate the inestimable value of what he has been given and to take responsibility for it: this fundamental principle must be placed at the center of one's reflection in order to clarify and solve the moral problems raised by artificial interventions on life as it originates and on the processes of procreation.

2. NEW TECHNOLOGIES=BETTER THERAPEUTIC RESOURCES+RISKS

Thanks to the progress of the biological and medical sciences, man has at his disposal ever more effective therapeutic resources; but he can also acquire new powers, with unforeseeable consequences, over human life at its very beginning and in its first stages. Various procedures now make it possible to intervene not only in order to assist but also to dominate the processes of procreation. These techniques can enable man "to take in hand his own destiny" but they also expose him "to the temptation to go beyond the limits of a reasonable dominion over nature." They might constitute progress in the service of man, but they also involve serious risks.

3. CHURCH AS "EXPERT IN HUMANITY"

Requests for clarification and guidance are coming not only from the faithful but also from those who recognize the Church as "an expert in humanity" with a mission to serve the "civilization of love" and of life.

4. CRITERIA OF MORAL JUDGMENT

These criteria are the respect, defense and promotion of man, his "primary and fundamental right" to life, his dignity as a person who is endowed with a spiritual soul and with moral responsibility and who is called to beatific communion with God.

5. SCIENCE WITHOUT CONSCIENCE LEADS TO MAN'S RUIN

The rapid development of technological discoveries gives greater urgency to this need to respect the criteria just mentioned: science without conscience can only lead to man's ruin. "Our era needs such wisdom more than bygone ages if the discoveries made by man are to be further humanized. For the future of the world stands in peril unless wiser people are forthcoming." (*Gaudium Et Spes,* #15)

6. THE NATURAL MORAL LAW

The natural moral law expresses and lays down the purposes, rights and duties which are based upon the bodily and spiritual nature of the human person. Therefore this law cannot be thought of as simply a set of norms on the biological level; rather it must be defined as the rational order whereby man is called by the Creator to direct and regulate his life and actions and in particular to make use of his own body.

7. POPE JOHN PAUL ON NORMS FOR NOT STRICTLY THERAPEUTIC PROCEDURES

Pope John Paul II forcefully reaffirmed this to the World Medical Association when he said: "Each human person, in his absolutely unique singularity, is constituted not only by his spirit, but by his body as well. Thus, in the body and through the body, one touches the person himself in his concrete reality. To respect the dignity of man consequently amounts to safeguarding this identity of the man 'corpore et anima unus', as the Second Vatican Council says (Gaudium et Spes, 14, par. 1). It is on the basis of this anthropological vision that one is to find the fundamental criteria for decision-making in the case of procedures which are not strictly therapeutic, as, for example, those aimed at the improvement of the human biological condition.''

8. LIMITS OF COMPETENCE OF BIOLOGISTS & DOCTORS

No biologist or doctor can reasonably claim, by virtue of his scientific competence, to be able to decide on people's origin and destiny. This norm must be applied in a particular way in the field of sexuality and procreation, in which man and woman actualize the fundamental values of love and life.

9. INTERVENTIONS MUST BE RESPECTFUL OF MAN/WOMAN/GOD MARRIAGE

God who is love and life, has inscribed in man and woman the vocation to share in a special way in his mystery of personal communion and in his work as Creator and Father. For this reason marriage possesses specific goods and values in its union and in procreation which cannot be likened to those existing in lower forms of life. Such values and meanings are of the personal order and determine from the moral point of view the meaning and limits of artificial interventions on procreation and on the origin of human life. These interventions are not to be rejected on the grounds that they are artificial. As such, they bear witness to the possibilities of the art of medicine. But they must be given a moral evaluation in reference to the dignity of the human person, who is called to realize his vocation from God to the gift of love and the gift of life.

Advances in technology have now made it possible to procreate apart from sexual relations through the meeting in vitro of germ-cells previously taken from the man and the woman. But what is technically possible is not for that very reason morally admissible. Rational reflection on the fundamental values of life and of human procreation is therefore indispensable for formulating a moral evaluation of such technological interventions on a human being from the first stages of his development.

10. TWO CRITERIA: LIFE OF HUMAN BEING CALLED INTO EXISTENCE AND SPECIAL NATURE OF TRANSMISSION OF LIFE IN MARRIAGE

The fundamental values connected with the techniques of artificial human procreation are two: the life of the human being called into existence and the special nature of the transmission of human life in marriage. The moral judgment on such methods of artificial procreation must therefore be formulated in reference to these values.

a) Physical life, with which the course of human life in the world begins, certainly does not itself contain the whole of a person's value, nor does it represent the supreme good of man who is called to eternal life. However it does constitute in a certain way the "fundamental" value of life, precisely because upon this physical life all the other values of the person are based and developed. The inviolability of the innocent human being's right to life from the moment of conception until death is a sign and requirement of the very inviolability of the person to whom the Creator has given the gift of life.

b) By comparison with the transmission of other forms of life in the universe, the transmission of human life has a special character of its own, which derives from the special nature of the human person. "The transmission of human life is entrusted by nature to a personal and conscious act and as such is subject to the all-holy laws of God: immutable and inviolable laws which must be recognized and observed. For this reason one cannot use means and follow methods which could be licit in the transmission of the life of plants and animals." (Pope John XXIII, Mater et Magistra)

11. ONLY SEXUAL REPRODUCTION BETWEEN SPOUSES IS ALLOWED

Human procreation requires on the part of the spouses responsible collaboration with the fruitful love of God; the gift of human life must be actualized in marriage through the specific and exclusive acts of husband and wife, in accordance with the laws inscribed in their persons and in their union.

Attempts or plans for fertilization between human and animal gametes and the gestation of human embryos in the uterus of animals, or the hypothesis or project of constructing artificial uteruses for the human embryo. . . . These procedures are contrary to the human dignity proper to the embryo, and at the same time they are contrary to the right of every person to be conceived and to be born within marriage and from marriage. Also, attempts or hypotheses for obtaining a human being without any connection with sexuality through "twin fission," cloning or parthenogenesis are to be considered contrary to the moral law, since they are in opposition to the dignity both of human procreation and of the conjugal union.

12. AN IMPORTANT QUESTION

Can one speak of a right to experimentation upon human embryos for the purpose of scientific research ? What norms or laws should be worked out with regard to this matter?

13. THE ISSUE. . .

Certainly no experimental datum can be in itself sufficient to bring us to the recognition of a spiritual soul; nevertheless, the conclusions of science regarding the human embryo provide a valuable indication for discerning by the use of reason a personal presence at the moment of this first appearance of human life: how could a human individual not be a human person? The Magisterium has not expressly committed itself to an affirmation of a philosophical nature, but it constantly reaffirms the moral condemnation of any kind of procured abortion. This teaching has not changed and is unchangeable.

14. EMBRYO MUST BE TREATED AS ANY OTHER HUMAN BEING

The human being is to be respected and treated as a person from the moment of conception; and therefore from that same moment his rights as a person must be recognized, among which in the first place is the inviolable right of every innocent human being to life. This doctrinal reminder provides the fundamental criterion for the solution of the various problems posed by the development of the biomedical sciences in this field: since the embryo must be treated as a person, it must also be defended in its integrity, tended and cared for, to the extent possible, in the same way as any other human being as far as medical assistance is concerned.

15. IS PRENATAL DIAGNOSIS MORALLY LICIT?

If prenatal diagnosis respects the life and integrity of the embryo and the human fetus and is directed towards its safeguarding or healing as an individual, then the answer is affirmative. But this diagnosis is gravely opposed to the moral law when it is done with the thought of possibly inducing an abortion depending upon the results: a diagnosis which shows the existence of a malformation or a hereditary illness must not be the equivalent of a death sentence.

16. IS EXPERIMENTATION ON HUMAN EMBRYOS LICIT?

Medical research must refrain from operations on live embryos, unless there is a moral certainty of not causing harm to the life or integrity of the unborn child and the mother, and on condition that the parents have given their free and informed consent to the procedure. No objective, even though noble in itself, such as a foreseeable advantage to science, to other human beings, or to society can in any way justify experimentation on living human embryos or fetuses, whether viable or not, either inside or outside the mother's womb. The practice of keeping alive human embryos in vivo or in vitro for experimental or commercial purposes is totally opposed to human dignity.

17. THE HEART OF THE MATTER IN IN VITRO FERTILIZATION (IVF) AND EMBRYO TRANSFER (ET)

The connection between in vitro fertilization and the voluntary destruction of human embryos occurs too often. This is significant: through these procedures, with apparently contrary purposes, life and death are subjected to the decision of man, who thus sets himself up as the giver of life and death by decree. This dynamic of violence and domination may remain unnoticed by those very individuals who, in wishing to utilize this procedure, become subject to it themselves. The facts recorded and the cold logic which links them must be taken into consideration for a moral judgment on IVF and ET (in vitro fertilization and embryo transfer): the abortion-mentality which has made this procedure possible thus leads, whether one wants it to or not, to man's domination over the life and death of his fellow human beings and can lead to a system of radical eugenics.

Nevertheless, such abuses do not exempt one from a further and thorough ethical study of the techniques of artificial procreation considered in themselves, abstracting as far as possible from the destruction of embryos produced in vitro.

18. HETEROLOGUS IN VITRO FERTILIZATION

Every human being is always to be accepted as a gift and blessing of God. However, from the moral point of view a truly responsible procreation vis-a-vis the unborn child must be the fruit of marriage.

For human procreation has specific characteristics by virtue of the personal dignity of the parents and of the children: the procreation of a new person, whereby the man and the woman collaborate with the power of the Creator, must be the fruit and the sign of the mutual self-giving of the spouses, of their love and their fidelity. The fidelity of the spouses in the unity of marriage involves reciprocal respect of their right to become a father and a mother only through each other.

The child has the right to be conceived, carried in the womb, brought into the world and brought up within marriage: it is through the secure and recognized relationship to his own parents that the child can discover his own identity and achieve his own proper human development.

The tradition of the Church and anthropological reflection recognize in marriage and in its indissoluble unity the only setting worthy of truly responsible procreation.

19. SOCIAL REASONS OBTAIN AS WELL

By reason of the vocation and social responsibilities of the person, the good of the children and of the parents contributes to the good of civil society; the vitality and stability of society require that children come into the world within a family and that the family be firmly based on marriage.

20. HETEROLOGOUS ARTIFICIAL FERTILIZATION NEVER ALLOWED

Heterologous artificial fertilization is contrary to the unity of marriage, to the dignity of the spouses, to the vocation proper to parents, and to the child's right to be conceived and brought into the world in marriage and from marriage.

Recourse to the gametes of a third person, in order to have sperm or ovum available, constitutes a violation of the reciprocal commitment of the spouses and a grave lack in regard to that essential property of marriage which is its unity.

Heterologous artificial fertilization violates the rights of the child; it deprives him of his filial relationship with his parental origins and can hinder the maturing of his personal identity. Furthermore, it offends the common vocation of the spouses who are called to fatherhood and motherhood: it objectively deprives conjugal fruitfulness of its unity and integrity; it brings about and manifests a rupture between genetic parenthood, gestational parenthood and responsibility for upbringing. Such damage to the personal relationships within the family has repercussions on civil society: what threatens the unity and stability of the family is a source of dissension, disorder and injustice in the whole of social life.

Furthermore, the artificial fertilization of a woman who is unmarried or a widow, whoever the donor may be, cannot be morally justified.

21. STERILITY DOES NOT OBVIATE THE NEGATIVE MORAL JUDGMENT

The desire to have a child and the love between spouses who long to obviate sterility which cannot be overcome in any other way constitute understandable motivations; but subjectively good intentions do not render heterologous artificial fertilization comformable to the objective and inalienable properties of marriage or respectful of the rights of the child and of the spouses.

22. IS SURROGATE MOTHERHOOD MORALLY LICIT?

No, for the same reasons which lead one to reject heterologous artificial fertilization: for it is contrary to the unity of marriage and to the dignity of procreation of the human person.

Surrogate motherhood represents an objective failure to meet the obligations of maternal love, of conjugal fidelity and of responsible motherhood; it offends the dignity and the right of the child to be conceived, carried in the womb, brought into the world and brought up by his own parents; it sets up, to the detriment of families, a division between physical, psychological and moral elements which constitute those families.

23. PRINCIPLES GOVERNING HOMOLOGOUS ARTIFICIAL FERTILIZATION

The Church's teaching on marriage and human procreation affirms the "inseparable connection, willed by God and unable to be broken by man on his own initiative, between the two meanings of the conjugal act: the unitive meaning and the procreative meaning. Indeed, by its intimate structure, the conjugal act, while most closely uniting husband and wife, capacitates them for the generation of new lives, according to laws inscribed in the very being of man and of woman." (Paul VI—Humanae Vitae)

The same doctrine concerning the link between the meanings of the conjugal act and between the goods of marriage throws light on the moral problem of homologous artificial fertilization, since "it is never permitted to separate these different aspects to such a degree as positively to exclude either the procreative intention or the conjugal relation." (Pius XII)

Richard Westley

Homologous artificial fertilization, in seeking a procreation which is not the fruit of a specific act of conjugal union, objectively effects an analogous separation between the goods and the meanings of marriage.

Thus, fertilization is licitly sought when it is the result of a ''conjugal act which is per se suitable for the generation of children to which marriage is ordered by its nature and by which the spouses become one flesh.'' (Canon 1061) But from the moral point of view procreation is deprived of its proper perfection when it is not desired as the fruit of the conjugal act, that is to say of the specific act of the spouses union.

The moral value of the intimate link between the goods of marriage and between the meanings of the conjugal act is based upon the unity of the human being, a unity involving body and spiritual soul. Spouses mutually express their personal love in the ''language of the body,'' which clearly involves both ''spousal meanings'' and parental ones. The conjugal act by which the couple mutually express their self-gift at the same time expresses openness to the gift of life. It is an act that is inseparably corporal and spiritual. It is in their bodies and through their bodies that the spouses consummate their marriage and are able to become father and mother. In order to respect the language of their bodies and their natural generosity, the conjugal union must take place with respect for its openness to procreation; and the procreation of a person must be the fruit and the result of married love. The origin of the human being thus follows from a procreation that is ''linked to the union, not only biological but also spiritual, of the parents, made one by the bond of marriage.'' (John Paul II) Fertilization achieved outside the bodies of the couple remains by this very fact deprived of the meanings and the values which are expressed in the language of the body and in the union of human persons.

The human person must be accepted in his parents' act of union and love; the generation of a child must therefore be the fruit of this mutual giving which is realized in the conjugal act wherein the spouses cooperate as servants not as masters in the work of the Creator who is love.

In reality, the origin of a human person is the result of an act of giving. The one conceived must be the fruit of his parents' love. He cannot be desired or conceived as the product of an intervention of medical or biological techniques; that would be equivalent to reducing him to an object of scientific technology. No one may subject the coming of a child into the world to conditions of technical efficiency which are to be evaluated according to standards of control and dominion.

The moral relevance of the link between the meanings of the conjugal act and between the goods of marriage, as well as the unity of the human being and the dignity of his origin, demand that the procreation of a human person be brought about as the fruit of the conjugal act specific to the love between spouses. The link between procreation and the conjugal act is thus shown to be of great importance on the anthropological and moral planes, and it throws light on the positions of the Magisterium with regard to homologous artificial fertilization.

24. IS HOMOLOGOUS 'IN VITRO' FERTILIZATION MORALLY LICIT?

The answer to this question is strictly dependent on the principles just mentioned. Certainly one cannot ignore the legitimate aspirations of sterile couples. For some, recourse to homologous IVF and ET appears to be the only way of fulfilling their sincere desire for a child. The question is asked whether the totality of conjugal life in such situations is not sufficient to ensure the dignity proper to human procreation. It is acknowledged that IVF and ET certainly cannot supply for the absence of sexual relations and cannot be preferred to the specific acts of conjugal union, given the risks involved for the child and the difficulties of the procedure. But it is asked whether, when there is no other way of overcoming sterility which is a source of suffering, homologous in vitro fertilization may not constitute an aid, if not a form of therapy, whereby its moral licitness could be admitted.

The desire for a child—or at the very least an openness to the transmission of life—is a necessary prerequisite from the moral point of view for responsible human procreation. But this good intention is not sufficient for making a positive moral evaluation of in vitro fertilization between spouses. The process of IVF and ET must be judged in itself and cannot borrow its definitive moral quality from the totality of conjugal life of which it becomes a part nor from the conjugal acts which may precede or follow it.

It has already been recalled that, in the circumstances in which it is regularly practiced, IVF and ET involves the destruction of human beings, which is something contrary to the doctrine on the illicitness of abortion previously mentioned. But even in a situation in which every precaution were taken to avoid the death of human embryos, homologous IVF and ET dissociates from the conjugal act the actions which are directed to human fertilization. For this reason the very nature of homologous IVF and ET always must be taken into account, even abstracting from the link with procured abortion.

Homologous IVF and ET is brought about outside the bodies of the couple through actions of third parties whose competence and technical activity determine the success of the procedure. Such fertilization entrusts the life and identity of the embryo into the power of doctors, biologists and establishes the domination of technology over the origin and destiny of the human person. Such a relationship of domination is in itself contrary to the dignity and equality that must be common to parents and children.

Conception in vitro is the result of the technical action which presides over fertilization. Such fertilization is neither in fact achieved nor positively willed as the expression and fruit of a specific act of the conjugal union. In homologous IVF and ET, therefore, even if it is considered in the context of 'de facto' existing sexual relations, the generation of the human person is objectively deprived of its proper perfection: namely, that of being the result and fruit of a conjugal act in which the spouses can become "cooperators with God for giving life to a new person."

These reasons enable us to understand why the act of conjugal love is considered in the teaching of the Church as the only setting worthy of human procreation. For the same reasons the so-called "simple case," i.e. a homologous

IVF and ET procedure that is free of any compromise with the abortive practice of destroying embryos and with masturbation, remains a technique which is morally illicit because it deprives human procreation of the dignity which is proper and connatural to it.

Certainly, homologous IVF and ET fertilization is not marked by all the ethical negativity found in extra-conjugal procreation; the family and marriage continue to constitute the setting for the birth and upbringing of the children. Nevertheless, in conformity with the traditional doctrine relating to the goods of marriage and the dignity of the person, the Church remains opposed from the moral point of view to homologous 'in vitro' fertilization. Such fertilization is in itself illicit and in opposition to the dignity of procreation and of the conjugal union, even when everything is done to avoid the death of the human embryo.

Although the manner in which human conception is achieved with IVF and ET cannot be approved, every child which comes into the world must in any case be accepted as a living gift of the divine Goodness and must be brought up with love.

25. WHAT ABOUT HOMOLOGOUS ARTIFICIAL INSEMINATION?

If the technical means facilitates the conjugal act or helps it to reach its natural objectives, it can be morally acceptable. If, on the other hand, the procedure were to replace the conjugal act, it is morally illicit.

Artificial insemination as a substitute for the conjugal act is prohibited by reason of the voluntarily achieved dissociation of the two meanings of the conjugal act. Masturbation, through which the sperm is normally obtained, is another sign of this dissociation: even when it is done for the purpose of procreation, the act remains deprived of its unitive meaning: "It lacks the sexual relationship called for by the moral order, namely the relationship which realizes 'the full sense of mutual self-giving and human procreation in the context of true love'." (Congregation of the Faith—Declaration on Certain Questions Concerning Sexual Ethics)

26. THE SUFFERING CAUSED BY INFERTILITY IN MARRIAGE

The suffering of spouses who cannot have children or who are afraid of bringing a handicapped child into the world is a suffering that everyone must understand and properly evaluate.

On the part of spouses, the desire for a child is natural: it expresses the vocation to fatherhood and motherhood inscribed in conjugal love. This desire can be even stronger if the couple is affected by sterility which appears incurable. Nevertheless, marriage does not confer upon the spouses the right to have a child, but only the right to perform those natural acts which are per se ordered to procreation.

A true and proper right to a child would be contrary to the child's dignity and nature. The child is not an object to which one has a right, nor can he be considered as an object of ownership: rather, a child is a gift, "the supreme gift" and the most gratuitous gift of marriage, and is a living testimony of the mutual giving of his parents. For this reason, the child has a right, as already mentioned, to be the fruit of the specific act of conjugal love of his parents; and he also has the right to be respected as a person from the moment of his conception.

Nevertheless, whatever its cause or prognosis, sterility is certainly a difficult trial. The community of believers is called to shed light upon and support the suffering of those who are unable to fulfill their legitimate aspiration to motherhood and fatherhood. Spouses who find themselves in this sad situation are called to find in it an opportunity for sharing in a particular way in the Lord's Cross, the source of spiritual fruitfulness. Sterile couples must not forget that "when procreation is not possible, conjugal life does not for this reason lose its value. Physical sterility in fact can be for spouses the occasion for other important services to the life of the human person, for example adoption, various forms of educational work, and assistance to other families and to poor or handicapped children." (John Paul II)

27. THE VALUES AND MORAL OBLIGATIONS THAT CIVIL LEGISLATION MUST RESPECT AND SANCTION IN THIS MATTER

The inviolable right to life of every innocent human individual and the rights of the family and of the institution of marriage constitute fundamental moral values, because they concern the natural condition and integral vocation of the human person; at the same time they are constitutive elements of civil society and its order.

For this reason the new technological possibilities which have opened up in the field of biomedicine require the intervention of the political authorities and of the legislator, since an uncontrolled application of such techniques could lead to unforeseeable and damaging consequences for civil society. Recourse to the conscience of each individual and to the self-regulation of researchers cannot be sufficient for insuring respect for personal rights and public order. If the legislator responsible for the common good were not watchful, he could be deprived of his prerogatives by researchers claiming to govern humanity in the name of the biological discoveries and the alleged "improvement" processes which they would draw from those discoveries. "Eugenism" and forms of discrimination between human beings could come to be legitimized: this would constitute an act of violence and a serious offense to the equality, dignity and fundamental rights of the human person.

28. CONCLUSION

The spread of technologies of intervention in the processes of human procreation raises very serious moral problems in relation to the respect due to the human being from the moment of conception, to the dignity of the person, of his or her sexuality, and of the transmission of life.

With this Instruction the Congregation for the Doctrine of the Faith, in fulfilling its responsibility to promote and defend the Church's teaching in so serious a matter, addresses a new and heartfelt invitation to all those who, by reason of their role and their commitment, can exercise a positive influence and insure that, in the family and in society, due respect is accorded to life and love. It addresses this invitation to those responsible for the formation of consciences and of public opinion, to scientists and medical professionals, to jurists and politicians. It hopes that all will understand the incompatibility between recognition of the dignity of the human person and contempt for life and love, between faith in the living God and the claim to decide arbitrarily the origin and fate of a human being.

In particular, the Congregation of the Faith addresses an invitation with confidence and encouragement to theologians, and above all to moralists, that they study more deeply and make ever more accessible to the faithful the contents of the teaching of the Church's Magisterium in the light of a valid anthropology in the matter of sexuality and marriage and in the context of the necessary interdisciplinary approach. Thus they will make it possible to understand ever more clearly the reasons for and the validity of this teaching. By defending man against the excesses of his own power, the Church of God reminds him of the reasons for his true nobility; only in this way can the possibility of living and loving with that dignity and liberty which derive from respect for the truth be insured for the men and women of tomorrow. The precise indications which are offered in the present Instruction therefore are not meant to halt the effort of reflection but rather to give it a renewed impulse in unrenounceable fidelity to the teaching of the Church.

In the light of the truth about the gift of human life and in the light of the moral principles which flow from that truth, everyone is invited to act in the area of responsibility proper to each and, like the good Samaritan, to recognize as a neighbor even the littlest among the children of men (Cf. Luke 10:29-37). Here Christ's words find a new and particular echo:—What you do to one of the least of my brethren, you do unto me'' (Matt. 25:40).

During an audience granted to the undersigned Prefect after the Plenary session of the Congregation for the Doctrine of the Faith, the Supreme Pontiff, John Paul II, approved this Instruction and ordered it to be published.

Given at Rome from the Congregation for the Doctrine of the Faith, February 22, 1987, the Feast of the Chair of St. Peter, the Apostle.

CHAPTER FIVE
Human Control of Life and Death

I GUESS I have to admit that I am not outraged at the thought of human control of the life/death processes. It does not strike me as necessarily a profanation of the human. Indeed, if one holds that such control is to be exclusively God's, my immediate reaction is to recall John F. Kennedy's remark that "God's work must truly be our own." Most Americans, I think, feel that way. That does not make it morally right, of course, but it gives some indication of why Americans are not readily disposed to accept the traditional Catholic stance of an absolute "hands-off" policy regarding life and death. To say that life and death are God's work alone, what I elsewhere called "the divine dominion principle"[1], strikes me as just too dogmatic and too simplistic a stance in the face of all the bio-medical advances of our time. Whatever immorality there be in such life/death decisions, it does not stem from the fact that a human being usurped a divine prerogative, but rather from the fact that they arose from a disordered intention and/or were carried out by improper means.

To say otherwise is to close one's eyes to the fact that science and technology have put in human hands decisions once left to God alone because of human impotence. It is to overlook the fact that God foresaw this development, and gave us intellect and reason nonetheless. The case could be made that God meant for the human race to mature and take a more active role in life/death issues. For in the end, it is not science or technology which ultimately empowers us, but God. Unless one takes that sort of position, there is nothing to be discussed from the Catholic perspective. Human beings are then simply interdicted from ever exercising control over life or death; end of discussion, case closed.

Having said that, let me immediately add, however, that the principles which lead the Catholic tradition to interdict all human control over life and death are still as true and as much of a gift to humankind as ever, even if one judges the divine dominion principle and the absolute interdiction drawn from it as a bit extreme. One has only to consider the present practices of genetic engineering to be convinced of it.

1. *Genetic Engineering: The Pros and Cons*

Ever since the advent of human life on this planet, human beings have viewed the world as there, ready-at-hand, to be used to facilitate survival and to achieve other human goals. We have "engineered" our world from the beginning, fashioning it into something more compatible with human life and purposes. As our knowledge of how nature worked expanded, our power to control our environment to suit ourselves increased, reaching its zenith perhaps in our ventures to outer space in the last half of this century. Still, that magnificent accomplishment was of a kind with the discovery of fire, the identification of the elements, and all the startling achievements of physics, chemistry and the industrial revolution.

Concomitant with our entry into space, the culminating event of the physical, chemical and industrial advances of humankind over the centuries, there occurred a biological discovery which portends to be the beginning of a whole new line of development, culminating in the twenty-first and twenty-second centuries in we know not what. But from all appearances, it will be a more profound change than any that has occurred in the millennia preceding it.

That biological discovery was the uncovering of the structure of a chemical that holds the secret to all biological life, the so-called DNA molecule, deoxyribonucleic acid. DNA holds the secret of life, containing as it does the instructions for producing everything from one-celled organisms to a human being with more than sixty trillion cells. If our engineering efforts up to this point were post-factum, that is accepting the givens of nature and re-ordering them for human purposes, we are now in a position to practice some a priori engineering on living matter, programming in advance what is given. Our potential to do that accounts for the fact that the discovery of DNA has been labeled the beginning of the "biological revolution," a revolution undoubtedly more significant than the industrial and electronic revolutions which preceded it.

Discovering DNA was only the first step, of course. In order to begin controlling life, a technology of breaking down the code into its various parts and then re-combining them in new combinations was required. Recombinant DNA technology is the key to increased control, and it has been quietly developing for the past thirty years. Genes, which are the equivalent of DNA, can be decoded, cut into identifiable segments, joined to other DNA in other organisms. The unbridgeable boundaries between various species no longer exist. The language of biology is universal, allowing science to join human, plant, animal, bacterial genes in order to achieve some desired result. The startling effects of this new technology have been making headlines in the past few years, thus galvanizing public opinion both pro and con.

Already we have bacteria which have been altered in their genetic code so as to produce human insulin. Interferon, the anti-viral cancer fighter, can now be produced in greater quantities in that same way. Plant and human genes can be isolated, extracted and grown in bacteria, where they multiply, giving scientists a reasonable supply of genetic protein to experiment with. In 1981 the first computerized "gene machine" was put on line. One types in the genetic code for a particular gene, and in a matter of hours the machine produces synthetic gene fragments that can be joined and inserted into the DNA of living organisms for experimental and therapeutic purposes. Of course the ultimate aim is to turn breeding (plant, animal and human) into an exact science, in which traits are engineered in advance (eugenics) rather than developed naturally through evolution. A second aim is to so manipulate human and animal cells to reveal the mechanisms that control their growth and development and the genetic disorders which bring on disease. That opens the door to gene alteration or replacement as a means of therapy. The genetic codes of plants and animals have already been altered in the hope of producing super-plants, and super-animals. Can super-humans be far behind?

The discovery of DNA and the successes already achieved in "engineering life" have reinforced the mechanistic view of life which arose at the height of the industrial revolution. Living organisms had always seemed less determined than inorganic matter which blindly and unconsciously follows the laws of physics and chemistry. But this is only an apparent difference since, as we have now come to know, living organisms are themselves machines developing according to a specific and determined inner blueprint. And just as human engineering of inorganic nature yielded spectacular results like space travel, so biological genetic engineering holds the promise of unheard of marvels in the next century, as humans learn to manipulate and control not only their environment but their own biological make-up as well.

In the face of such advances, it becomes more and more difficult to think of living things as individual members of discrete species. Rather we are all, in this view, just bundles of genetic information. Bundles of information which shall eventually be able to be re-programmed for our own purposes, thanks to science. The questions of the sacredness of life, and of the appropriate limits on scientific and technological manipulation of life, will cease to arise as a new post-biological-revolution ethics emerges.

We are not yet there. So voices of dissent can still be heard in the land, questioning the wisdom and morality of the path which the new biology seems determined to follow. And as was true with regard to the reproductive technologies, the dissent comes from common human reason, as well as from the various religious traditions.

Common human reason first questions the wisdom of the marriage between the new biology and business. The splitting of DNA and the recombining of the isolated elements in new combinations, as was the case with the splitting of the atom, has given rise to whole new industries which seek to capitalize on the new technologies. But corporations, unlike professions like science and medicine, must give primary consideration to "the bottom line," i.e. profit. Having invested large sums of money to develop new strains of microbes and bacteria, and to amass precious quantities of the new by-products such genetically altered organisms produce, big business is eager to get on with marketing their new "products." It seeks the protection of government and law by seeking and getting patents on the "new life" it has created. But it grows impatient with delays necessitated by government regulations and testing, and the temptation to bribe and dissemble in order to get the show on the road is great. Experience shows that under such circumstances, governmental control is weak and ineffective, and caution is thrown to the winds in order to more quickly capitalize on investment. Put succinctly, our recent experience with pollution and the handling of toxic and nuclear wastes, and the now customary corporate subversion of government regulations and public officials, shows that it is not very prudent to look to corporations to safeguard the common human good.

Secondly, introducing altered microbes into the environment is a very risky business. Unlike chemicals, living things cannot be controlled once in the environment. It seems foolhardy to put the ecology of the earth at risk out of ignorance. We simply don't know what effect genetically altered bacteria will have on the environment. Acting in haste, for profit's sake, and out of ignorance because of impatience we quite simply *don't really know what it is we are doing*. We have no way to estimate the long-term effects of this new technology. Still we forge ahead, naively led on by the startling beneficial results already achieved to assume that the results will always be beneficial or, if not, the benefits achieved will always offset any detrimental effects produced. But the fact is, we just don't know. Thus the assurances of the scientists and the corporations have the hollow ring of self-interest to them. With the memory of a similar scenario recently played out in the nuclear power industry, common human reason questions the prudence and morality of putting life on the planet at risk by acting out of ignorance.

But undoubtedly the most serious concern of common human reason about the new genetic technologies is the specter it raises of human eugenics. The technologies which allow us to genetically alter plants and animals for our own purposes can be used to alter the human gene pool as well. Since DNA, the blueprint for all organic life, is the same, animal and plant husbandry can easily lead to human husbandry. Indeed, that is the expressed goal of genetic engineering, to eventually improve the genetic constitution of human beings. All the work and research on cells, proteins, bacteria and microbes leads, many fear, by its own inner logic, to research on human beings. This seems to be going too far and to exceed appropriate limits, recalling to mind as it does Hitler and the Nazi experiments on humans during World War II aimed at producing a pure Aryan strain of human beings.

As we have already seen, technologies once in place seem to have a life of their own, since they are available for uses other than the original one. So, though genetic alterations can be therapeutic, alleviating genetic disorders in humans, it is not easy to separate the therapeutic from the eugenic. Put otherwise, it is one thing to alter genes to treat specific identifiable genetic disease, it is another thing to alter them not to correct disorder and disease, but to achieve some characteristics deemed important to the culture. Now while those may be different enterprises from the "moral" point of view, they are on a continuum of eugenic improvement of the race. Common human reason is wary of putting such power in the hands of scientists and corporations, not to mention what a government might be able to do to its population with that technology.

a. *Genetic Engineering: The Catholic Perspective*

And as has always been the case, in the forefront of the battle to respect the dignity and nobility of all life, but especially human life, is the Catholic church. It welcomes the concern of public human reason into the struggle, which it so often finds itself waging alone and unheeded. Indeed, at the end of the Congregation for the Doctrine of the Faith document on respect for human life, it invites governments to exercise some control over the present situation, and not to rely simply on the conscience or good will of individuals.

> Recourse to the conscience of each individual and to the self-regulation of researchers cannot be sufficient for ensuring respect for personal rights and public order. If the legislator responsible for the common good were not watchful, he could be deprived of his prerogatives by researchers claiming to govern humanity in the name of the biological discoveries and the alleged ''improvement'' process which they would draw from those discoveries. ''Eugenism'' and forms of discrimination between human beings could come to be legitimized: this would constitute an act of violence and a serious offense to the equality, dignity and fundamental rights of the human person.[2]

In that statement, the ''divine dominion principle'' is not invoked, as it is elsewhere in the document[3], because it is addressed to governments which contain many non-believers. The argument is couched in terms of Western culture's oft proclaimed commitment to human equality and dignity. To an age which at least verbally rails against discrimination, the church brands eugenism as the ultimate manifestation of that vice. Those without certain desired genetic qualities are viewed as "less than acceptable," and this through no fault of their own. To discrimination for reasons of race, color or gender, is now added discrimination by reason of ones genes. And to those who say that the manipulation of genetic material is not in itself eugenic, the church warns that without real vigilance and control there is no way of preventing genetic research from turning into a radical eugenics.[4]

To those who reject any justifiable limit on human activity, the church appears once again to be a cranky naysayer. To them, the document gently and pastorally remarks:

> By defending man against the excesses of his own power, the Church of God reminds him of the reasons for his true nobility; only in this way can the possibility of living and loving with that dignity and liberty which derive from respect for the truth be insured for the men and women of tomorrow.[5]

Our science and technology have put awesome power in our hands. We are smart enough to unlock the secrets of matter and of life, but are we wise enough to keep from using that power beyond the bounds of right reason and right order? The voices of the Catholic church and of common human reason are joined in trying to defend humankind from the excesses of its own power in the matter of genetic engineering. For what we do in this area of research and technology will affect not only the lives of the present generation, but of unborn generations yet to come. It is the height of irresponsibility for us to simply push ahead out of self-interest, unmindful and uncaring of those who will inherit our mistakes, and have to live them as we will not.

As for the revisionist perspective, it would echo the official church position on all but one issue, that of divine dominion. When the traditional Catholic position says that controlling life is God's prerogative and that it is *never* allowed that human beings be so bold as to usurp that prerogative, it is really saying that such acts are in themselves objectively evil. But as has been shown, according to the revisionists there are no acts which are in themselves morally evil, because acts do not become part of the moral universe until the human will and intention are factored in. But as we have also seen, it is possible to argue against eugenics without invoking the divine dominion principle. Indeed, the Congregation for the Faith did exactly that at key points in its 1987 document. Revisionists have no difficulty whatsoever seconding that kind of moral reasoning, because it rests on the very principles of proportionality between human intention and right order, and between human ends and the means chosen to achieve them which they take to be central. So apart from the slight demure regarding "divine dominion," the Catholic tradition is at one in its moral assessment of genetic engineering, especially as it promises to be applied to human beings. Affirming of the truly therapeutic use of such technology, our tradition categorically rejects as disordered and immoral its eugenic use.

Life, Death and Science

2. *Organ Transplants: The Pros and Cons*

The past twenty years have seen the birth, and the maturing of organ transplant technology. It is, perhaps, the most rapidly improving of the new technologies. We can all remember when most people who received transplanted organs died shortly thereafter, but new surgical techniques and the discovery of new and more effective immuno-suppressive drugs allow ever greater numbers of transplant patients to not only survive, but to lead normal lives. The sight of planes and helicopters rushing the organs of fatal accident victims to hospitals across the country where critically ill patients await the "gift of life" is played out regularly on TV news programs. Organ transplants have become, in the last quarter of the twentieth century, if not quite commonplace, at least no longer extraordinary. Obviously, this technology is here to stay. And given its brief and spectacularly successful history, it seems a bit stodgy, at this late date, to raise questions about the morality of the enterprise.

Actually, however, the questions which common human reason raises concerning organ transplants have been present from the beginning. It is just that they have not always been addressed and so continue to be raised by rational women and men of good will. While there may certainly be nothing disordered about a particular life-saving transplant operation, the medical strategy of organ transplantation in our health care delivery system as a whole is not without its moral dilemmas. At the very least, the whole issue is beset with troublesome ambiguities. For organ transplant technology creates the need for suitable organs, and because organs are transplantable only under certain very optimum conditions, a pressure is generated to take donor organs from persons not yet dead according to the long accepted medical and legal definitions of "death." A new definition of "death" is therefore being forged expressly to respond to and accommodate transplant technology. The new concept of "brain death" allows for the removal of organs while the heart is still pumping, better insuring the suitability of donor organs for transplant. This has special application in the cases of anencephalic babies. This move to a new definition of "death" has profound societal effects and brings into question the traditional ways of respecting human life. Once again, we see a widely accepted, valuable and therapeutic technology precipitating moral life/death dilemmas for the culture in which it arose.

But, of course, that is not the whole story. There are over 200,000 people in the United States awaiting transplants. Of these, 35 percent, or about 70,000 are waiting for a vital organ such as a heart, kidney, liver, lung, pancreas or bone marrow. They are in life-threatening situations. The rest are waiting for corneas, bone, middle ear bone, skin, connective tissue and the like. Though not in a life-threatening condition, these people's lives would be greatly enhanced by the availability of donor organs. Americans are urged to donate their body organs to help such people, and to "give the gift of life." The technology is remarkable, but no less remarkable in this materialistic culture of ours is the growing number of people who voluntarily donate their organs to help others. What could be more respectful of life and the truly human? It seems strangely unfitting in this self-centered age of ours to reject, in the name of morality, this miracle of human graciousness.

Of course, giftedness is not the issue. The problematic issues center on the possible abuses generated by the widespread need for organs. With human organs in short supply, there is immense pressure to procure them, and enterprising individuals would, left to themselves, turn trafficking in human organs into a very lucrative business. And as with surrogate mothers, the poor and disadvantaged are then tempted to sell their organs. That started to happen, so in 1984, Congress, to nip the problem in the bud, passed a law, the Uniform Anatomical Gift Act (UAGA), prohibiting the selling of human organs for transplant. It also prohibits the automatic "taking" of organs by health care professionals, requiring them to get voluntary consent from the donor, or his next of kin. The aim was to keep the human body and its parts from becoming "property" and hence commodities on the open market. Many applauded the wisdom of that decision at the time as being respectful of human rights and dignity, but such a decision necessarily did nothing to alleviate the severe shortage of transplantable organs. Those who urge the selling of organs, to give incentive to potential donors, think that the 1984 law actually has contributed to the shortage. But as of now, they have been unsuccessful in changing the law of the land, which remains committed to retaining the "gift" dimension of donor organs.

A second problematic area has to do with the wisdom of expending so much of our health care resources on saving the lives of a select few who can afford such operations, when so many in our culture have no access to minimal adequate health care. Given the fact of limited resources, is the transplant program really the wisest way to use them?

Is it really moral and just under the circumstances? This raises an issue which is beyond the scope of our considerations here. The issue of whether minimal health care is a service and a right of all, or whether it is a commodity subject, like all commodities, to the economic laws of supply and demand. While the Congress has done little to stop the inexorable movement of health care from a profession to a business, to its credit it has insisted that human organs are not for sale, and that when it comes to human body parts the inherent dignity of the human being can only be preserved if organ donation is freely and graciously chosen by the donor. Some may die for want of available transplantable organs, but better that should happen than that the door should be opened to putting us all at risk of having organs taken without our consent, or even against our wills.

a. *Redefining "Death" to Alleviate the Problem*

Before the new technology the legal definition of death, forged through generations of judicial decisions, was based on signs which could be easily observed and detected, i.e. the ceasing of all bodily functions, especially heart beat, blood flow and respiration. With the development of sophisticated life support systems, it became clear that cardiopulmonary activity might well be sustained by drugs and machines and the patient be, for all intents and purposes, dead. By the late 1960's medical research had reached the point of being able to discern a complete absence of brain functions, and that this was as accurate a sign of death for patients on life support systems as the old cardiopulmonary signs were for those who were not. Indeed, both sets of signs pointed to exactly the same physiological condition, and both were equally accurate.

In 1968, an Ad Hoc Committee of the Harvard Medical School attempted to address the problem of the definition of "death," and expressly gave as one of its reasons that "obsolete criteria for the definition of death can lead to controversy in obtaining organs for transplantation."[6]

That was not the only reason to undertake such a task; the major reason given was that under the old definition of death, attempts were made to resuscitate patients who were really dead and thus remained forever after comatose, thus filling hospital beds which were needed by others. In any event, the attempt to re-define death was done primarily to decrease the burden of human suffering, on patients and their families. Put simply, the startling improvement in resuscitation technology is not entirely a boon and a blessing. It has also increased the number of patients who are resuscitated only to be "vegetables," i.e. permanently comatose. The Harvard Committee tried to contribute to alleviating this problem by proposing new criteria for death by giving a clinical definition of irreversible coma.

Since any organ which no longer functions and has no possibility of functioning can be said to be "dead," the problem the Harvard Committee set for itself was to determine the characteristics of a permanently non-functioning brain.[7] First, there is a total unresponsiveness both to external stimuli and internal needs. Even the most painful stimuli evoke no response. Second, there are no spontaneous muscular movements of any kind for at least an hour or more, including respiration. This can be easily determined even if the patient is on a respirator. Third, the absence of central nervous system activities, including blinking, corneal, pharyngeal and tendon reflexes. Fourth, there is an absolutely flat electroencephalogram. And finally, these tests must be redone after a 24 hour period with no discernible change in any of the signs.

When *all* these signs are present, the Harvard Committee concludes, the patient is for all intents and purposes dead, may be declared so, and if the patient is on life support, only *then* may it be turned off. The declaration of death at that juncture has two significant effects: it relieves the medical team of any further obligation to attempt resuscitation; and if the patient or his family have voluntarily donated organs they may be taken while still in optimum condition for transplanting.

Many object to this new definition of death, seeing it simply as a pragmatic move on the part of the medical profession to find a way to take transplantable organs from "live" patients. Others claim that since we can never be absolutely certain beyond all question that such a state as that described by the Harvard Committee actually is irreversible, citing cases of prolonged coma thought to be irreversible from which the patient emerged after a long period of time, it would be morally wrong to act on the Committee's criteria.

One of the inherent difficulties in defining death is that it is hard for us to conceive of it other than as a momentary event. We expect it to be clearly identifiable. But no definition of death is without its critics, because no matter how hard we try to isolate the instant or moment of death, we seem unable to do it. James Rachels uses an analogy to make that very point. The relation between "dying" and "death" is analogous to traveling towards a destination and arriving there. To ask for the exact moment of death is like asking for the exact moment at which an air traveler arrives in Philadelphia. He writes:

> Exactly when does an air traveler arrive in Philadelphia? When the airplane first broaches the space over the city? When the plane

> touches the airport runway? When the passenger sets foot off the plane? It seems arbitrary which moment we designate the moment of arrival, nevertheless, the concept of arrival is the concept of a momentary event.[8]

The concept ''death,'' Rachels thinks, is just like that. It too is a ''concept'' of a momentary event, but in fact it is somewhat arbitrary what we stipulatively agree to designate as the moment of death, just as it is arbitrary as to which moment in the process we call the moment of ''arrival'' in Philadelphia. Prior to the advent of all the new medical technology, we stipulated that the stopping of respiration, heartbeat and blood flow was the moment of death. Now we are reasonably sure that someone can be quite dead and still have those properties due to the advent of new drugs and life support machines. The fact of the matter is that dying is a process, and human beings have always arbitrarily designated one or other moment of that process as ''the moment of death.'' Since that has always been the case, and since no single moment could ever definitively be designated as the moment of death, it is entirely appropriate that, in the light of the new technology, we designate some other moment as ''the moment of death.'' But we must remember that our newly designated moment is no less arbitrary and no more sacred than those which have preceded it, and that as we learn more and our technology gets better we shall undoubtedly come up with yet another definition of ''death.''

Admittedly, the new definition of death is aimed at relieving families of having ''brain dead'' relatives kept on expensive machines for prolonged periods of time, allowing as it does the medical team to ''pull the plug'' should the Harvard Committee criteria be met. As for the impact of the definition on the organ transplant situation, it does make possible the taking of organs in optimum condition, but according to the the law of the land, the Uniform Anatomical Gift Act (UAGA), prior voluntary consent is still required. So the number of available transplantable organs still remains a function of people's willingness to give the "gift of life." While the number of us willing to do that is growing, it is still painfully small and hence far below the number of those who need organs.

By the late 1970's the need for new and uniform legislation recognizing the standard cardiopulmonary criteria for death but adding the new "brain death" criteria as well was universally felt. So after almost two decades of work the Uniform Determination of Death Act (UDDA) was finally passed by Congress in 1982. It has been subsequently adopted in eighteen states, and similar legislation adopted in twenty others, and the highest courts in four other states have explicitly recognized the new neurological criteria. So both sets of criteria for determining death are now pretty much the law of the land.

b. *Anencephalic Fetuses/Infants & Organ Donation*

But no sooner had the UDDA been passed than pressure began to mount to alter it to accommodate the special and tragic case of anencephalic children. Such children lack the major brain structures, being genetically deformed so that they possess only a brain stem. The life expectancy of such children is anywhere from one or two days to one or two weeks. But they all die very soon after birth, and are, as far as we can tell, barely sensate.

Due to the new in utero diagnostic techniques, it is possible for a woman to determine whether the fetus she is carrying is anencephalic. To an expectant mother the news that she is must be devastating. The joys of giving life and birthing are supplanted by a profound sense of tragedy and hopelessness. Many opt to abort such fetuses rather than bring them to term. But some couples will not succumb to death, will not let death be the last word for their child, the fruit of their love. In a gracious gesture, out of their pain, they choose to bring the child to term, and to donate the healthy organs of their severely deformed and doomed child to "give life and hope" to other babies whose lives can be saved only by receiving a donor organ. In the midst of their own tragedy, such couples opt to give the "gift of life." And they choose to do it because it is the only way they can make sense of and find meaning in the situation. That decision gives the woman the courage to continue on in her pregnancy even though she knows she carries death within her, for out of that tragic death she has found a way to bring life.

Those who try to find solace in their personal tragedy that way soon discover that it is not so easy to give the "gift of life" these days. Two great institutions stand against them, the government with its Uniform Determination of Death Act (UDDA), and the church with its divine dominion principle. It is not that either institution is against "gift giving," rather it is the very special way in which the gift has to be given in the case of anencephalics which causes them concern.

Anencephalics, for some as yet unknown reason, do not develop the higher brain structures, the hemispheres, and are left with only a brain stem. As already stated, their life expectancy if they manage to come to term at all (most anencephalic infants are stillborn), is from one or two days to one or two weeks. All die very soon after birth. How soon? Each case is different and there is no way to know in advance. That means that if they are to be permitted to donate their organs, they have to be put on life support systems immediately at birth. They are now being kept alive, not for any therapeutic reason since their fate is already sealed, but for the good of possible organ recipients. They are being "used" as means for another's end. Generally, that alone would be enough to render the act immoral. But things get even more complicated.

Once on life support, the question arises as to when it would be permissible to "harvest" the organs of the anencephalic neonate. According to the Uniform Determination of Death Act (UDDA), that cannot be until either cessation of all cardiopulmonary activity, or, using the criterion added in 1982, the cessation of all brain activity. But the anencephalic neonate has a brain stem, and so long as it remains active controlling cardiopulmonary activity, the child cannot be legally declared dead. Once the lower brain centers stop working and all cardiopulmonary activity ceases, the child may be declared legally dead according to the UDDA, but at that point its organs are most likely not suitable for transplant. Should the physicians obey the law, there is no way the grieving couple can bring life out of the death of their child. Should they accede to the couple's wishes, they will violate the UDDA and are subject to prosecution and the loss of their license to practice medicine. That's the dilemma.

To relieve this situation, it is being suggested that the Uniform Determination of Death Act (UDDA) be amended to expressly exclude anencephalic children, allowing a special set of criteria to be applied to this very special class of neonates. In effect, what is being suggested is that the criteria "cessation of *all* brain activity" not apply to anencephalics, and that because of their very special condition they be declared legally dead at birth. They would then be put on life support systems at birth, their organs harvested within a reasonable time, certainly within two weeks, after which they will be respectfully buried. All this, of course, on the assumption of the consent of the parents, in accord with the Uniform Anatomical Gift Act (UAGA).

The legal battle over whether to amend the UDDA in behalf of anencephalic children and their parents will undoubtedly go on for some years. In the meantime, of course, science and technology will continue to progress and develop new strategies and techniques for dealing with organ donors in general and anencephalics in particular, thus precipitating still further moral dilemmas around the life/death issues. In the midst of all this ambiguity and confusion, physicians and patients must make moral decisions *now.* They cannot wait for the last word to be spoken on the matter. In every age, for the sake of those who must make difficult decisions now, the Catholic church has always taken a clear stand and given good counsel. It continues in that tradition in our day.

c. *Organ Transplants: The Catholic Perspective*

In many ways, the whole concept of "donor organs" is very much in keeping with the highest aspirations of the Catholic church. It is a symbol of giftedness which witnesses to the gracious generosity of God, who is the author and Lord of life. As has been suggested, there are obviously no moral dangers there, and the church applauds the new life saving organ transplant technology. But the church warns that this very technology has created a situation in which the temptation to violate human dignity and rights, and to use our life saving powers beyond proper limits is very great. The manipulation of life and death in order to "harvest human organs"is a violation of right order and a serious profanation of the life of some for the benefit of others. But God, not humankind, is the Lord of life and death, and acts which put that power in human hands cannot be condoned.

Not only is it always immoral for one to take direct action to forcibly end innocent human life against the will of the victim, it is always immoral to do it even with the victim's consent. Indeed, one may not take any direct action against one's own life. And the reason in all three cases is quite clear, it is a blatant usurpation of a divine prerogative by a creature. St. Thomas writes:

> To kill oneself is never allowed because life is a gift to man from God who alone has the authority to kill and to give life. Hence whoever takes his own life sins against God in the same way that he who kills another's slave sins against the slave's master, and as he sins who takes on himself for judgment a matter not entrusted to him.[9]

And again:

> That a person has dominion over himself is because he is endowed with free choice. Thanks to that free choice a man is at liberty to dispose of himself with respect to those things in this life which are subject to his freedom. But the passage from this life to a hap-

> pier one is not one of those things, for one's passage from this life is subject to the will and power of God.[10]

Invoking the "divine dominion principle" with such absoluteness and energy, the traditional Catholic position cannot possibly condone attempts to harvest human organs so long as the donor is "still alive." Indeed, the traditional view does not find it easy to accept even the concept of "brain death," since prior to a donor's being really dead, i.e. cessation of all cardiopulmonary and brain activity, any life ending action would be a gravely disordered and immoral act.

Unable on its own principles to be really accepting even of the "brain death" criteria of the Harvard Committee, the Catholic tradition sees attempts to further loosen those criteria in the case of anencephalics, allowing the harvesting of their organs while there is still brain stem and cardiopulmonary activity as nothing short of advocating the murder of some for the benefit of others. It is an unthinkable profanation of human life, to be neither advocated nor done. Modern science and technology would be better advised to use its genius and power to find a way to use the donor organs of those declared dead on the traditional criteria, rather than to seek looser criteria in order to harvest organs from donors judged still "living" by those same criteria. When human beings start to play God about life and death, it puts all of us at risk and none is safe.

3. *Some Concluding Remarks Concerning Life and Death*

However generally right-headed and wise the counsel of the Catholic church in these life/death matters may be, two sorts of cases especially lead many both within and without the church to demure. No matter how strongly and fervently the Catholic church rehearses the traditional position, good and God-fearing people continue to question whether in the cases of mercy-killing and anencephalic children there might not be another position equally in accord with Christian faith. The church continues to say no. But goodly numbers of believers still wonder whether it might not be so. What are we to make of this?

One possibility, of course, is to take a rather ultra-conservative approach by saying that the Magisterium of the church has spoken on these issues and that is the end of it. If one cannot in conscience follow the counsel of the Magisterium on life/death issues, one is openly defiant of authority and honesty and authenticity require her to leave the church. That has always been the conservative answer on such issues.[11]

Another possibility is to see the Magisterium as giving good counsel on moral matters, but leaving room for individual conscience and what the Lord of life is revealing to believers in their daily experiences. It had always been traditional, up until the time of the definition of papal infallibility at Vatican Council I (1870), that there were *two* living sources of the truths of faith, not just one. The Magisterium of the church, and the Consensus fidelium, those things all or the vast majority of Catholics believe out of their lived experience. With the definition of papal infallibility, the Consensus fidelium began to decline as a vital source of Catholic truth. Until in our day, the Magisterium alone claims to be the source of Catholic truth. A very untraditional position to be sure, in light of the more long standing tradition that the teaching church (Magisterium) can only teach what the believing church (Consensus fidelium) already believes.[12]

One cannot help but wonder, then, what the future holds for

Catholics with regard to the "divine dominion principle." As more and more Catholics come to experience the agony of prolonging life beyond the time of its death, as they experience the request of their terminally ill loved ones to be liberated from the very technology we have been discussing because it no longer gives life but dehumanizes them, the Lord of life will reveal to them the truth of the matter. As that revelation becomes communally funded within the Catholic community, it will become more and more awkward for the Magisterium to teach against its own believing people. Obviously, we are not there yet. But if one had to predict the direction things will go, that would be the prediction. Since we are not there yet, let me simply cite the words of St. Thomas More on the issue, confident that in the twenty-first century it will become the standard Catholic position.

> If a disease is not only incurable but also distressing and agonizing without any cessation, then the priests and the public officials exhort the man, since he is now unequal to all life's duties, a burden to himself, and a trouble to others, and is living beyond the time of his death, to make up his mind not to foster the pest and plague any longer nor to hesitate to die now that life is a torture to him but, relying on good hope, to free himself from this bitter life as from prison and the rack, or else voluntarily to permit others to free him. In this course he will act wisely, since by death he will put an end not to enjoyment but to torture. Because in doing so he will be obeying the counsels of the priests, who are God's interpreters, it will be a pious and holy action. Those who have been persuaded by these arguments either starve themselves to death or, being put to sleep, are set free without the sensation of dying. *But they do not make away with anyone against his will,* nor in such

> a case do they relax in the least their attendance upon him. They believe that death counseled by authority is honorific.[13]

As we come to the end, let me say something on this issue in my own name. I have written on this issue twice before[14] over the span of almost a decade. Nothing has transpired in those years to cause me to change my assessment of the matter. I think that St. Thomas Aquinas was wrong and that St. Thomas More got it exactly right. And the reason I do, is because I take Thomas Aquinas seriously when he says that "life is a gift of God to man." It is a gift to us, it is truly ours, not something we hold on inter-library loan. And precisely because life is God's gift to us, we hold it without strings or conditions. Aquinas notwithstanding, we are at liberty to dispose of our lives. And though I would not want to counsel suicide to anyone, I do not see how it can be gravely immoral for a human being to take her own life in the conditions outlined by Thomas More. I know that at present the bulk of the Catholic community thinks otherwise, but I foresee the day when that will no longer be the case. In the past, pneumonia mercifully delivered people from their agony. The new drugs and technology prevent that happening, so people will do what is required so as not to be dehumanized. Of that we can be sure. For some time to come they will be judged to have acted immorally, but eventually God's truth will prevail. Until then we must possess our souls in patience, and live in fear and trembling at the life/death decisions we will be forced to make, trusting that the God who made us will understand our predicament.

Some new light is cast on the case of anencephalic children if we invoke this "gift principle" rather than the "divine dominion principle" about human life. Freed from having to view that situation as the premature taking of a human life and as an usurpation of a divine prerogative, we are at liberty to see it as our instincts tell us it is, a grace-filled and truly human event.

If the life of the anencephalic child is truly its own, and if, as we saw in discussing fetal experimentation, proxy consent by parents is entirely appropriate in experimental as well as therapeutic situations, then we can assume that those same principles apply in its case. As the revisionist, Richard McCormick, pointed out, if we respect the full human dignity of the fetus, we must take into account not only its rights but also its normal human obligations. Especially the obligation to relate beneficently to others. Doomed as it is from the start, with no chance at life, but with a chance to give life, what might the anencephalic child want to do? If we assume that it is at liberty to dispose of its own life, might we not also assume that there is nothing wrong with its opting to make a gift of itself for others? To say otherwise, while it may better conform to the present Magisterium, is just too counter-intuitive. Our God is the God of abundant gifts, and it seems he would surely understand and applaud such graciousness on the part of one of his creatures. He affirmed and applauded such graciousness in Jesus by raising him up after the cross, why would we ever think he would do less for any one of us who did likewise?

But such differences among Catholics are really not all that significant when one considers how at one we are with respect to speaking out against the profanations of the human in our time. We can be very proud to be Catholic in these days. As it has done down through the ages, the Catholic church continues to speak to the moral concerns of people, bringing its traditional moral wisdom and common human reason to bear on the pressing issues of the day. Some may judge the Catholic position to be just a bit too rigid in spots, but behind the perceived rigidity is a real compassion and concern to protect the humanity of us all. For in the end, though the technology may be new, what constitutes right order in the new circumstances brought on by the new technology is really very much the same as it has always been. The limits of what we humans may morally do may be pushed back a bit, but the basic limitations remain because we are finite and human. The Catholic church has an uncanny record of correctly discerning in every age where those limits lie. We disregard her counsel at our own peril.

NOTES TO CHAPTER V

1. Cf. Chp. IV, "Justifying The Unthinkable," in May & Westley, *The Right to Die,* Thomas More, 1980, pp. 80-100.

2. *Instruction on Respect for Human Life . . .*, op. cit., p. 35.

3. *Ibid.*, p. 18.

4. *Ibid.*, p. 21.

5. *Ibid.*, p. 39.

6. "A Definition of Irreversible Coma: A Report of the Ad Hoc Committee of The Harvard Medical School," *Journal of the American Medical Association,* Vol. 205, No. 6 (August 1968), pp. 337-340.

7. This is commonly called "brain death," but the Harvard Committee avoided that terminology and spoke of this state as one of irreversible coma.

8. James Rachels, *The End Of Life: Euthanasia and Morality,* Oxford University Press, New York, 1986, p. 43.

9. *Summa Theologiae* I-II, 64, 5, c.

10. *Summa Theologiae* I-II, 64, 5, ad 3.

11. Ultra-conservatives take the same position with regard to the Magisterium's stand on contraception and birth control. Yet on that issue the majority of Catholics around the world disagree with the Magisterium. On the mercy-killing issue, the majority of Catholics still agree with the Magisterium, but a growing minority of exemplary believers do not. At stake here is the question of whether or not to be Catholic one must on each and every issue agree with the Magisterium. Rome might wish the answer to that were in the affirmative, but its teaching is that it is not. What *is* required of Catholics is that in forming their own consciences they take the position of the Magisterium seriously and respectfully into consideration. And should they not agree, they at least are not to publicly teach against the Magisterium. So, it would seem, those who demand absolute and total obedience to each and every edict of the Magisterium are more "Catholic" than the church which does not require that.

12. This principle was obviously violated in Paul VI's encyclical *Humanae Vitae,* on birth control. And because it was violated so blatantly, the teaching Church now finds itself in the awkward position of trying to proclaim against the faith of its people. All of which accounts for the deep division in the Church on that issue.

13. *Utopia,* ed. Edward Surtz, S.J., Yale University Press, New Haven, 1964, pp. 108-109.

14. May & Westley, *The Right to Die,* Thomas More, Chicago, 1980, and Dick Westley, *Morality and Its Beyond,* Twenty-Third Publications, Mystic, 1984, pp. 239-246.

BIBLIOGRAPHY

I. *General Works in Bio-Medical Ethics*

Abrams, N. & Buckner, M.D., *Medical Ethics: A Textbook and Reference for the Health Care Profession,* MIT Press, Cambridge, 1983.

Ashley, B. & O'Rourke K., *The Ethics of Health Care,* Catholic Health Assoc. of United States, St. Louis, Missouri, 1986.

Bellah, Robert, *Habits of the Heart,* Harper & Row, New York, 1985.

Bloom, Allan, *The Closing of the American Mind,* Simon & Schuster, New York, 1987.

Boulton, Wayne G., *Is Legalism A Heresy?,* Paulist Press, New York, 1982.

Colen, B.D., *Hard Choices: Mixed Blessings of Modern Medical Technology,* Putnam's, New York, 1986.

Craig, Middleton, & O'Connell eds., *Ethics Committees: A Practical Approach,* Catholic Health Assoc. of United States, St. Louis, Missouri, 1986.

Edelstein, Ludwig, "The Hippocratic Oath: Text, Translation and Interpretation," *Bulletin of the History of Medicine, Supplement 1,* Johns Hopkins Press, Baltimore, 1943.

Edwards, R.B & Graber, G.C., *Bio-Ethics,* Harcourt Brace Jovanovich, New York, 1988.

Engelhardt, H. Tristam Jr., *The Foundations of Bioethics,* Oxford University Press, New York, 1986.

Fagothey, Austin, S.J., *Right And Reason,* C.V. Mosby, St. Louis, 1963.

Feldman, David M., *Health And Medicine In the Jewish Tradition: l'Hayyim—to life,* Crossroad, New York, 1986.

Freeman, John M., *Tough Decisions: A Casebook In Medical Ethics,* Oxford Univ. Press, New York, 1987.

Goldstein, Doris Mueller, *Bioethics: A Guide To Information Sources,* Gale Research Co., Detroit, Michigan, 1982.

Goldworth, Amnon, *The Moral Limit To Private Profit in Entrepreneurial Science,* Hastings Center Report, Vol. 17, No.3, June 1987, pp. 8-10.

Gorovitz, S., "Ethical Dilemmas in Medicine: Who Should Decide?," *National Forum,* 58, no. 2, 1978, 3.

Harron, Burnside & Beauchamp, *Health And Human Values: A Guide To Making Your Own Decisions,* Yale University Press, New Haven, 1983.

Hastings Center Report—Special Supplement—*Biomedical Ethics: A Multinational View,* Hastings Center Report, Vol. 17, No. 3, June, 1987, pp. 1-36.

Jonsen, Siegler, & Winslade, *Clinical Ethics: A Practical Approach To Ethical Decisions in Clinical Medicine,* Macmillan, New York, 1986.

Kass, Leon R., *Toward a More Natural Science: Biology and Human Affairs,* The Free Press, New York, 1985.

Kass, Leon R., "Thinking About the Body," *Hastings Center Report,* Vol. 15, February, 1985, pp. 20-30.

Kelly, Margaret John, *Justice and Health Care,* Catholic Health Assoc. of United States, St. Louis, Missouri, 1985.

Kieffer, George, *Bioethics: A Textbook of Issues,* Addison-Wesley, Reading, Mass., 1979.

Leach, Gerald, *The Biocrats,* McGraw Hill, New York, 1970.

Lockwood, Michael ed., *Moral Dilemmas in Modern Medicine,* Oxford University Press, New York, 1985.

Lomasky, Loren E., *Public Money, Private Gain, Profit For All* Hastings Center Report, Vol. 17, No. 3, June 1987, pp. 5-7.

Macklin, Ruth, *Mortal Choices: Bioethics in Today's World,* Pantheon Books, New York, 1987.

Maguire, Daniel C., *Moral Choice,* Doubleday, New York, 1978.

McCarthy, D.G. & Bayer, E.J. eds., *Handbook On Critical Life Issues,* Pope John Center, St. Louis, 1982.

McCormick, Richard A., S.J., *How Brave a New World: Dilemmas in Bioethics,* Doubleday, Garden City, N.Y., 1981.

Mendelsohn, Swazey, & Taviss, *Human Aspects of Bio-Medical Innovation,* Harvard Univ. Press, Cambridge, Mass., 1971.

Menzel, Paul T., *Medical Costs, Moral Choices: A Philosophy of Health Care Economics In America,* Yale University Press, New Haven, 1983.

O'Reilly, Sean, *Bioethics and The Limits of Science,* Christendom Publications, Front Royal, Va., 1980.

Opposing Viewpoints Pamphlets, *What Ethical Standards Should Guide The Health Care System,* Greenhaven Press, St. Paul, 1987.

Pellegrino, E. & Thomasma D., *A Philosophical Basis of Medical Practice: Toward A Philosophy and Ethic of the Healing Professions,* Oxford University Press, New York, 1981.

President's Commission for the, *Study of Ethical Problems in Medicine & Biomedical & Behavioral Research: Making Health Care Decisions,* Government Printing Office, Washington, D.C., 1982.

Rosner, Fred, *Modern Medicine and Jewish Ethics,* Yeshiva University Press, New York, 1986.

Shannon, Thomas, *Bioethics,* Paulist Press, New York, 1987.

Sharman, Veatch & Fenner, *Bibliography of Society, Ethics and the Life Sciences,* Hastings Institute, Hastings, N.Y., 1975.

Utke, Allen R., *Bio-Babel: Can We Survive The New Biology?,* John Knox Press, Atlanta, 1978.

VanDeVeer, D. & T. Regan eds., *Health Care Ethics: An Introduction,* Temple University Press, Philadelphia, 1986.

Varga, Andrew C., *The Main Issues in Bioethics,* Paulist Press, New York, 1980.

Walters, LeRoy, *Bibliography of Bioethics,* Gale Research, Detroit, Michigan, 1975.

Weiss, Ann E., *Bioethics: Dilemmas in Modern Medicine,* Enslow Publishers, Hillside, N.J., 1985.

II. *On Being a Physician*

Bulger, Roger J. ed., *In Search of the Modern Hippocrates,* University of Iowa Press, Iowa City, 1987.

Carlton, Wendy, *In Our Professional Opinion: The Primacy of Clinical Judgment Over Moral Choice,* University of Notre Dame Press, Notre Dame, Ind., 1978.

Gorovitz, Samuel, *Doctors' Dilemmas: Moral Conflict and Medical Care,* Macmillan, New York, 1982.

May, William F., *The Physician's Covenant: Images of the Healer In Medical Ethics,* Westminster Press, Philadelphia, 1983.

Pellegrino, E.D., "Toward a Reconstruction of Medical Morality: The Primacy Profession and the Fact of Illness," *Journal of Medical Philosophy,* 4, 1979, 32.

III. *Life Death Issues*

Annas, George J., "Quinlan, Saikewicz, and Now Brother Fox," *Hastings Center Report,* 10, June, 1980.

Black, P.M., "Clinical Problems in the Use of Brain-Death Standards," *Archives of Internal Medicine,* 143, 1983, 121-123.

Collins, V.U., "Limits of Medical Responsibility in Prolonging Life: Guides to Decisions," *American Medical Association Journal,* 206, 1968.

Heifetz, Milton D., *The Right To Die: A Neurosurgeon Speaks Of Death With Candor,* Putnam, New York, 1975.

Humphrey, Derek, *Let Me Die Before I Wake: Hemlock's Book of Self-Deliverance for the Dying,* Grove Press, New York, 1984.

Imbus, S.H. & Zawacki, B.E., "Autonomy for Burned Patients When Survival is Unprecedented," *New England Journal of Medicine,* 297, 1977, 308.

Jackson, D. & Youngner, S., "Patient Autonomy and 'Death with Dignity': Some Clinical Caveats," *New England Journal of Medicine,* 301 No. 8, Aug. 23, 1979.

Ladd, John ed., *Ethical Issues Relating to Life and Death,* Oxford University Press, New York, 1981.

Larue, Gerald A., *Euthanasia And Religion: A Survey of the Attitudes of World Religions to the Right-To-Die,* Hemlock Society, Los Angeles, 1985.

Lynn, Joanne ed., *By No Extraordinary Means: The Choice to Forgo Life-sustaining Food and Water,* Indiana University Press, Bloomington, 1986.

Maestri, William, *Choose Life and Not Death: A Primer on Abortion, Euthanasia, and Suicide,* Alba House, New York, 1986.

Maguire, Daniel C., *Death By Choice,* Doubleday, Garden City, N.Y., 1984.

May, W. & Westley, R., *The Right To Die,* Thomas More, Chicago, 1980.

McCormick, R. & Hellegers, A., "The Specter of Joseph Saikewicz: Mental Incompetence and the Law," *America,* April 1, 1978.

Rachels, James, *The End of Life: Euthanasia and Morality,* Oxford University Press, New York, 1986.

Relman, A.S., "The Saikewicz Decision: Judges as Physicians," *New England Journal of Medicine,* 298, 1978, 508.

Robertson, John A., *The Rights of the Critically Ill: The Basic ACLU Guide To the Rights of Critically Ill and Dying Patients,* Ballinger Publishing Co., Cambridge, Mass., 1983.

Showalter, J. & Andrew, B., *To Treat or Not To Treat: A Working Document For Making Critical Life Decisions,* Catholic Health Assoc. of United States, St. Louis, Missouri, 1984.

Simmons, Paul D., *Birth and Death: Bioethical Decision Making,* Westminster Press, Philadelphia, 1983.

Veatch, R.M., *Death, Dying and the Biological Revolution,* Yale University Press, New Haven, 1976.

Walton, Douglas N., *On Defining Death: An Analytic Study Of The Concept of Death In Philosophy and Medical Ethics,* McGill-Queen's University Press, Montreal, 1979.

Walton, Douglas N., *Brain Death: Ethical Considerations,* Purdue University Press, West Lafayette, Ind., 1980.

Weir, Robert F. ed., *Ethical Issues In Death and Dying,* Columbia Univ. Press, New York, 1986.

Wilson, Jerry B., *Death By Decision: The Medical, Moral and Legal Dilemmas of Euthanasia,* Westminster Press, Philadelphia, 1975.

Winslade, William J., *Choosing Life or Death: A Guide For Patients, Families, and Professionals,* Free Press, New York, 1986.

IV. *Abortion*

Butler,J.D. & Walbert, D.F. eds., *Abortion, Medicine, And The Law,* Facts On File Publications, New York, 1986.

Callahan, S. & Callahan, D. eds., *Abortion: Understanding Differences,* Plenum Press, New York, 1984.

Collins, Carol C., *Abortion: The Continuing Controversy,* Facts On File, New York, 1986.

Westley, Richard, *What A Modern Catholic Believes About The Right To Life,* Thomas More, Chicago, 1973.

V. *Human Reproduction*

Bayles, Michael D., *Reproductive Ethics,* Prentice Hall, Englewood Cliffs NJ, 1984.

Callahan, Daniel et al, "In Vitro Fertilization: Four Commentaries," *Hastings Center Report,* Vol. 8, October 1978, 7-14.

Council for Science & Society, *Human Procreation: Ethical Aspects of the New Techniques,* Oxford Univ. Press, New York, 1984.

Fromer, Margot Joan, *Ethical Issues in Sexuality and Reproduction,* Mosby, St. Louis, 1983.

Jones, David Gareth, *Brave New People: Ethical Issues At The Commencement of Life,* Eerdmans, Grand Rapids, Mich., 1985.

Keane N., & Breo, D., *Surrogate Mother,* Dodd Mead & Co., New York, 1981.

McCormick, Richard A. "Fetal Research, Morality and Public Policy," Hastings Center Report, Vol. 5, 1975.

McCullagh, Peter John, *The Foetus As Transplant Donor: Scientific, Social and Ethical Perspectives,* Wiley, New York, 1987.

O'Donovan, Oliver, *Begotten Or Made?,* Oxford University Press, New York, 1984.

Opposing Viewpoints Pamphlets, *Should Limits Be Placed On Reproductive Technology?,* Greenhaven Press, St. Paul, 1987.

Ozar, David, "The Case Against Thawing Unused Frozen Embryos," *Hastings Center Report,* 1985.

Schneider, Edward D. ed., *Questions About the Beginning of Life,* Augsburg Press, Minneapolis, 1985.

Singer, P. & Wells, D., *Making Babies: The New Science and Ethics of Conception,* C. Scribner's Sons, New York, 1985.

Walters, A. & Singer P. ed., *Test-Tube Babies,* Oxford University Press, Melbourne, 1982.

VI. *Neonates*

Amer. Acad. of Pediatrics, "Treatment of Critically Ill Newborns," *Pediatrics,* 72, No. 4, October 1983, 565-566.

Kuhse, Helga & Singer, Peter, *Should The Baby Live?: The Problem of Handicapped Infants,* Oxford University Press, New York, 1985.

Murray, T.H. & Caplan A.L. eds., *Which Babies Shall Live?: Humanistic Dimensions Of The Care of Imperiled Newborns,* Humana Press, Clifton, N.J., 1985.

Rhoden, Nancy K., "Treatment Dilemmas for Imperiled Newborns: Why Quality of Life Counts," *Southern California Law Review,* 58, no. 6, September 1985, 1283 ff.

Shelp, Earl E., *Born To Die?: Deciding The Fate of Critically Ill Newborns,* Free Press, New York, 1986.

Weir, Robert, *Selective Nontreatment of Handicapped Newborns,* Oxford University Press, New York, 1984.

VII. *Genetic Engineering*

Applebaum, E. & Kirestein, S., *A Genetic Counseling Casebook,* Free Press, New York, 1983.

Cherfas, Jeremy, *Man-made Life: An Overview of the Science, Technology and Commerce of Genetic Engineering,* Pantheon Books, New York, 1982.

Constantini, F. & Jaenisch, R., *Genetic Manipulation of the Early Mammalian Embryo,* Cold Spring Harbor Laboratory, Cold Spring Harbor, N.Y, 1985.

Fletcher, Joseph, *The Ethics of Genetic Control,* Doubleday, Garden City, N.Y., 1974.

Gaylin, Willard, "Genetic Screening: The Ethics of Knowing," *New England Journal of Medicine,* 286, June 22, 1972.

Glover, Jonathan, *What Sort of People Should There Be?,* Penguin Books, New York, 1984.

Goodfield, G.J., *Playing God: Genetic Engineering And The Manipulation Of Life,* Random House, New York, 1977.

Haring, Bernard, *Ethics of Manipulation: Issues in Medicine, Behavior Control And Genetics,* Seabury Press, New York, 1975.

Harris, Maureen ed., *Early Diagnosis of Human Genetic Defects,* U.S. Gov't Printing Office, Washington, D.C., 1972.

Hutton, Richard, *Bio-Revolution: DNA and the Ethics of Man-made Life,* New American Library, New York, 1978.

Langone, John, *Human Engineering, Marvel or Menace?,* Little Brown, Boston, 1978.

Menditto, Joseph, *Genetic Engineering, DNA and Cloning,* Whitston Publishing Co., Troy, New York, 1983.

Opposing Viewpoints Pamphlets, *Is Genetic Engineering Ethical?,* Greenhaven Press, St. Paul, 1987.

President's Commission for the, *Study of Ethical Problems in Medicine & Biomedical and Behavioral Research: Screening & Counseling For Genetic Conditions,* United States Printing Office, Washington, D.C., 1983.

President's Commission for the, *Study of Ethical Problems In Medicine &*

Biomedical & Behavioral Research: Ethical Issues of Genetic Engineering, Government Printing Office, Washington, D.C., 1982.

Ramsey, Paul, *Fabricated Man: The Ethics of Genetic Control,* Yale University Press, New Haven, 1970.

Rifkin, Jeremy, *Algeny,* Foundation On Economic Trends, 1983.

Rifkin, Jeremy, *Declaration of a Heretic,* Routledge & Kegan Paul, Boston, 1985.

VIII. *Experimentation*

Beecher, Henry K., "Experimentation in Man," *American Medical Association Journal,* 165, No. 5, 1959.

Nicholson, Richard J. ed., *Medical Research With Children: Ethics, Law and Practice,* Oxford University Press, New York, 1986.

Opposing Viewpoints Pamphlets, *Should Animals Be Used In Scientific Research?,* Greenhaven Press, St. Paul, 1987.

Ramsey, Paul, "Shall We 'Reproduce'? The Medical Ethics of In Vitro Fertilization," *Journal of the American Medical Association,* Vol. 220, No. 10, June 5, 1972.

Silverman, William A., *Human Experimentation: A Guided Step Into the Unknown,* Oxford University Press, New York, 1985.

IX. *Transplantation*

Annas, George J., "From Canada with Love: Anencephalic Newborns as Organ Donors," *Hastings Center Report,* Vol. 17, December 1987, pp. 36-38.

Capron, Alexander Morgan, "Anencephalic Donors: Separate the Dead From The Dying," *Hastings Center Report,* Vol. 17, February 1987, pp. 5-9.

Mistichelli, Judith Adams ed., *Baby Fae: Ethical Issues Surrounding Cross-species Organ Transplantation,* Kennedy Institute of Ethics, Georgetown Univ., 1985.

Opposing Viewpoints Pamphlets, *Are Organ Transplants Ethical?,* Greenhaven Press, St. Paul, 1987.

X. *Theological Accounts*

Congregation For The Doctrine Of The Faith, *Instruction On Respect For Human Life In Its Origin And On The Dignity of Procreation: Replies To*

Life, Death and Science

Certain Questions Of The Day, United States Catholic Conference, Washington, D.C., 1987. (Publication #156-3)

Congregation For The Doctrine Of The Faith, *Declaration On Certain Problems of Sexual Ethics,* in Austin Flannery, O.P., *Vatican Council II: More Post Concilar Documents,* Costello Publishing, Northport, New York, 1982, pp. 486-499.

Hauerwas, Stanley, *Suffering Presence: Theological Reflections on Medicine, the Mentally Handicapped, and the Church,* University of Notre Dame Press, Notre Dame, 1986.

Lammers, S.E. & Verhey, A. eds., *On Moral Medicine: Theological Perspectives In Medical Ethics,* Eerdmans, Grand Rapids, Mich., 1987.

Mahoney, John, *Bio-Ethics and Belief: Religion and Medicine in Dialogue,* Christian Classics, Westminster, Md., 1984.

Nelson, J. Robert, *Human Life: A Biblical Perspective for Bioethics,* Fortress Press, Philadelphia, 1984.

Shelp, Earl E. ed., *Theology And Bioethics: Exploring The Foundations and Frontiers,* D. Reidel, Boston, 1985.

Smith, David H., *Health And Medicine In the Anglican Tradition: Conscience, Community, and Compromise,* Crossroad, New York, 1986.

Westley, Dick, *A Theology of Presence: A Search for Meaning in American Catholic Experience,* Twenty-Third Publications, Mystic, 1988.

__________. *Morality And Its Beyond,* Twenty-Third Publications, Mystic, 1984.